The
Educator Wellness

PLAN
BOOK &
JOURNAL

Continuous Growth for Each Season
of Your Professional Life

Tina H. Boogren
Timothy D. Kanold
Jasmine K. Kullar

Solution Tree | Press
a division of
Solution Tree

555 North Morton Street
Bloomington, IN 47404
800.733.6786 (toll free) / 812.336.7700
FAX: 812.336.7790
email: info@SolutionTree.com
SolutionTree.com

Visit **go.SolutionTree.com/educatorwellness** to download the free reproducibles in this book.

Printed in the United States of America

Library of Congress Cataloging-in-Publication Data

Names: Boogren, Tina., author. | Kanold, Timothy D., author. | Kullar, Jasmine K., 1976- author.
Title: The educator wellness plan book and journal : continuous growth for each season of your professional life / Tina H. Boogren, Timothy D. Kanold, Jasmine K. Kullar.
Description: Bloomington, IN : Solution Tree Press, 2023. | Includes bibliographical references.
Identifiers: LCCN 2023012934 (print) | LCCN 2023012935 (ebook) | ISBN 9781958590492 (spiral bound) | ISBN 9781958590508 (ebook)
Subjects: LCSH: Teachers--Health and hygiene. | Educators--Health and hygiene. | Teachers--Mental health. | Educators--Mental health. | Well-being.
Classification: LCC LB3415 .B66 2023 (print) | LCC LB3415 (ebook) | DDC 371.1001/9--dc23/eng/20230411
LC record available at https://lccn.loc.gov/2023012934
LC ebook record available at https://lccn.loc.gov/2023012935

Solution Tree
Jeffrey C. Jones, CEO
Edmund M. Ackerman, President

Solution Tree Press
President and Publisher: Douglas M. Rife
Associate Publishers: Todd Brakke and Kendra Slayton
Editorial Director: Laurel Hecker
Art Director: Rian Anderson
Copy Chief: Jessi Finn
Senior Production Editor: Sarah Foster
Copy Editor: Madonna Evans
Proofreader: Charlotte Jones
Text and Cover Designer: Rian Anderson
Acquisitions Editor: Hilary Goff
Assistant Acquisitions Editor: Elijah Oates
Content Development Specialist: Amy Rubenstein
Associate Editor: Sarah Ludwig
Editorial Assistant: Anne Marie Watkins

To our fellow paper planner lovers,

We hope you pull out all your fancy pens, tabs, sticky notes, and stickers
to make this feel like your favorite planner yet.

May it help you live your very best life, season after season.

Acknowledgments

The concept for this *The Educator Wellness Plan Book and Journal* was birthed in a restaurant discussion based on the enthusiasm and passion Tina and Jasmine share for paper planners. Add in our desire to provide you with more than fifty-five strategies for your weekly wellness walk, and the wellness and paper planner merger was off and running!

When we presented the idea of a plan book and journal to complement our Wellness Solutions for Educators™ work to the Solution Tree publishing team, they immediately stepped up to help us accelerate out production timeline. As authors, we have produced more than thirty-five books with Solution Tree and stand in deep appreciation for their deep respect and care for our work. Thus, our deepest thanks go to Douglas Rife, Sarah Payne-Mills, Todd Brakke, and Kendra Slayton! Special thanks to Jeff Jones as well, whose belief in supporting our work as authors is only surpassed by his incredibly supportive actions.

A book like this requires what seems like an unending amount of time, drafts, rewrites, and more. If it reads and presents its space well, it is only because of the lead editor and her editorial team. Special, special thanks to Sarah Foster, who cares about this topic as much as we do, and who gave so much of her own time and wisdom to make the book fluid and complete for you. Thanks to Laurel, Rian, Jessi, Madonna, Charlotte, Hilary, Elijah, Amy, Sarah, and Anne Marie from the gifted Solution Tree editorial team!

We would also like to thank our reviewers extraordinaire: Brandon Jones, Janel Keating, Erin Lehman, Mark Onuschek, Dan Phelps, and Adrienne Turner. They gave us special insight and wisdom on how this book can be used, the value of its weekly invitations and tools for the reader, and how we could make it stronger in both form and substance.

Finally, we want to thank you for taking the time to choose *this* plan book, read and write your way through it, and for giving yourself the gift of wellness through your personal self-care and self-compassion. It is true. Our profession has its challenging moments and exhausting days. It also has the incredible opportunity to impact the lives of so many. To overcome that exhaustion and experience, the joy of that impact requires an intentional examination and a positive daily response to your health and well-being.

May this book, with its four seasons (dimensions) of wellness and its twelve months (routines) for improvement, help you live your best life every week as you plan for learning while simultaneously embracing new strategies for your wellness and well-being each day!

Visit **go.SolutionTree.com/educatorwellness**
to download the free reproducibles in this book.

Table of Contents

Reproducibles are in italics

Acknowledgments V
About the Authors XIII

PART 1
About This Plan Book and Journal I
Welcome 3
How to Use This Plan Book and Journal 5
    Educator Wellness Work 5
    Season-by-Season Planning and Wellness Work 6
    Monthly Work and Calendar 7
    Weekly Planners, Invitations, and Reflections 7
    The Why 8

PART 2
Summer: A Season of Renewal II
Summer Overview and Reflection:
Physical Wellness 12

JUNE
    Calendar 14
    June: Food and Hydration Routines 16
    Week One: Commit to Healthier Food Choices 18

Week Two: Increase Your Water Intake 20
Week Three: Commit to Eating Healthy Meals 22
Week Four: Focus on Eating Without Distractions 24
Week Five: Monitor Food's Effect on Mood 26
End-of-Month Reflection: Food and Hydration Routines 28

JULY
Calendar 30
July: Movement Routines 32
Week One: Track Your Sitting Time 34
Week Two: Find Time for Your Favorite Movement Activity 36
Week Three: Move 150 Minutes This Week 38
Week Four: Find a Partner for the 70,000 Steps Challenge . . . 40
Week Five: Schedule Movement Activities 42
End-of-Month Reflection: Movement Routines 44

AUGUST
Calendar 46
August: Sleep and Rest Routines 48
Week One: Track How Much You Sleep 50
Week Two: Create a Wind-Down Routine 52
Week Three: Incorporate Sleep Strategies 54
Week Four: Track Rest Time 56
Week Five: Incorporate Purposeful Rest 58
End-of-Month Reflection: Sleep and Rest Routines 60

End of Summer: What's Next? 62

PART 3
Fall: A Season of Opportunity

Fall: A Season of Opportunity 65

Fall Overview and Reflection: Mental Wellness . . 66

SEPTEMBER
Calendar 68
September: Decision Routines 70
Week One: Track Decisions 72
Week Two: Create Daily Habits 74
Week Three: Establish Boundaries Around Worktime 76
Week Four: Schedule Time for You 78
Week Five: Develop Self-Compassion 80
End-of-Month Reflection: Decision Routines 82

OCTOBER
Calendar 84
October: Balance Routines 86
Week One: Track Daily Activities 88
Week Two: Track Your Energy 90

Week Three: Track Verbal Communications. 92
Week Four: Eliminate Inputs and Noise 94
Week Five: Ask for Feedback 96
End-of-Month Reflection: Balance Routines 98

NOVEMBER

Calendar. 100
November: Efficacy Routines 102
Week One: Smile More 104
Week Two: Engage in a Strengths Challenge 106
Week Three: Create a Vision Board 108
Week Four: Start a Personal Résumé 110
Week Five: Learn Something New 112
End-of-Month Reflection: Efficacy Routines 114

End of Fall: What's Next? 116

PART 4
Winter: A Season of Perseverance 119

Winter Overview and Reflection: Emotional Wellness 120

DECEMBER

Calendar. 122
December: Awareness Routines 124
Week One: Track Daily Emotions 126
Week Two: Monitor Emotional Responses 128
Week Three: Share Pleasant Emotions 130
Week Four: Observe Emotional Impact 132
Week Five: Get Emotional Response Feedback 134
End-of-Month Reflection: Awareness Routines 136

JANUARY

Calendar. 138
January: Understanding Routines 140
Week One: Identify Pleasant Emotion Triggers 142
Week Two: Identify Unpleasant Emotion Triggers 144
Week Three: Identify Emotion Patterns 146
Week Four: Commit to Healthy Emotional Responses 148
Week Five: Model Healthy Emotional Responses 150
End-of-Month Reflection: Understanding Routines 152

FEBRUARY

Calendar. 154
February: Mindfulness Routines. 156
Week One: Notice React Versus Respond 158
Week Two: Practice Mindful Breathing 160

Week Three: Practice Meditation 162
Week Four: Experiment With Journaling. 164
Week Five: Take a Mindful Walk. 166
End-of-Month Reflection: Mindfulness Routines 168

End of Winter: What's Next? 170

PART 5
Spring: A Season of Transition 173

Spring Overview and Reflection: Social Wellness . 174

MARCH

Calendar. 176
March: Relationship Routines 178
Week One: Write Thank-You Notes 180
Week Two: Go for a Walk and Talk 182
Week Three: Write a Gratitude Note 184
Week Four: Build Relationship With a Colleague 186
Week Five: Identify Inner Circle 188
End-of-Month Reflection: Relationship Routines 190

APRIL

Calendar. 192
April: Trust Routines. 194
Week One: Avoid Gossip 196
Week Two: Listen Without Interruption 198
Week Three: Show Vulnerability by Apologizing 200
Week Four: Ask for Help 202
Week Five: Model and Build Trust 204
End-of-Month Reflection: Trust Routines 206

MAY

Calendar. 208
May: Purpose Routines. 210
Week One: Discover Who You Are as an Educator 212
Week Two: Consider Your Desires as an Educator 214
Week Three: Identify Your Purpose as an Educator 216
Week Four: Connect to Your Purpose. 218
Week Five: Share Your Purpose. 220
End-of-Month Reflection: Purpose Routines 222

End of Spring: What's Next? 224

APPENDIX A
Journal Tools 227

Weekly Tools Index 228
Healthy Snacks List 230
Water Tracker 231
Healthy Meals Planner 232
Food Choice and Impact on Mood 233
Time Spent Sitting and Impact on Mood 234
List of Movement Activities 235
Movement Minutes Tracker 236
70,000 Steps Challenge 237
Movement Activity Tracker 238
Sleep Tracker 239
Wind-Down Routine 240
Rest-Time Tracker 241
Decision Tracker 242
Daily Habit and Routine Commitments 243
Brainstorm Activities That Are Just for You 244
Your Daily Affirmations 245
Busy or Hurried Tracker 246
Positive Energy State Tracker 247
Verbal Communications Tracker 248
Eliminate Inputs and Noise Tracker 249
Record of Feedback 250
Strengths Challenge 251
My Vision Board 252
Personal TA-DA of Accomplishments 253
Emotions Tracker 254
Unpleasant Emotions Response Tracker 255
Pleasant Emotions Tracker 256
Impact of Your Emotions on Others 257
Emotional Response Feedback 258
Pleasant Emotion Triggers 259
Unpleasant Emotion Triggers 260
My Daily Challenge Commitment 261
I'm Grateful For 262
React Versus Respond Reflections 263
Journal Experimenting 264
Mindful Walking Emotions 265
Thank-You Notes 266
Gratitude Note 267
My Inner Circle 268
Listening Without Interrupting 269
Apology Reflections 270
Taking Initiative 271

Who Are You as An Educator? *272*

What Are Your Deepest Desires as an Educator?. *273*

What Is Your Purpose as an Educator? *274*

Connect to Your Purpose as an Educator *275*

APPENDIX B
Wellness Solutions for Educators
Rating, Reflecting, Goal Setting, Planning, and Progress Monitoring Protocol 277

Physical Wellness Dimension. 279

Mental Wellness Dimension 280

Emotional Wellness Dimension 281

Social Wellness Dimension 282

Educator Wellness Planning Tool—Strengths 283

Educator Wellness Planning Tool—Routines for Improvement . . . 284

Educator Wellness Goal Setting, Planning, and Progress Monitoring . 285

Educator Wellness Goal Setting, Planning, and Progress Monitoring . 286

REFERENCES AND RESOURCES . . 287

About the Authors

Tina H. Boogren, PhD, is a fierce advocate for educators and an award-winning educator, bestselling author, and highly sought-after speaker. Dr. Boogren has proudly served as a classroom teacher, mentor, instructional coach, and building-level leader and has presented for audiences all over the world.

Dr. Boogren is deeply committed to supporting educators so that they can support their students. She conducts highly requested and inspiring keynotes, workshops, and virtual webinars that focus on quality instruction, coaching, mentoring, and educator wellness, and she hosts a weekly podcast, *Self-Care for Educators With Dr. Tina H. Boogren.* Additionally, she is codirector of Solution Tree's Wellness Solutions for Educators with Dr. Timothy D. Kanold.

Dr. Boogren was a 2007 finalist for Colorado Teacher of the Year and was a recipient of her school district's Outstanding Teacher Award eight years in a row, from 2002 to 2009. Global Gurus recognized her as one of the top thirty Global Gurus in education. In addition, she is the author of numerous books, including *In the First Few Years: Reflections of a Beginning Teacher; Supporting Beginning Teachers; The Beginning Teacher's Field Guide: Embarking on Your First Years; 180 Days of Self-Care for Busy Educators; Take Time for You: Self-Care Action Plans for Educators,* which was the Independent Publisher Book Award gold winner in the education category; and *Coaching for Educator Wellness: A Guide to Supporting New and Experienced Teachers.* She is a coauthor of *Educator Wellness: A Guide for Sustaining Physical, Mental, Emotional, and Social Well-Being* with Timothy D. Kanold and *Motivating and Inspiring Students: Strategies to Awaken the Learner* with Robert J. Marzano, Darrell Scott, and Ming Lee Newcomb, and is a contributor to Richard Kellough and Noreen Kellough's *Middle School Teaching: A Guide to Methods and Resources,* Robert J. Marzano's *Becoming a Reflective Teacher,* and *Women Who Lead: Insights, Inspiration, and Guidance to Grow as an Educator,* edited by Janel Keating and Jasmine K. Kullar.

Dr. Boogren holds a bachelor's degree from the University of Iowa, a master's degree with an administrative endorsement from the University of Colorado Denver, and a doctorate in educational administration and policy studies from the University of Denver, and she is a Level 1 Certified Nutrition Coach and Specialist in Change Psychology through Precision Nutrition.

To learn more about Dr. Boogren's work, follow her @THBoogren on Twitter and Instagram, join her Facebook group (www.facebook.com/selfcareforeducators), and listen to her podcast, *Self-Care for Educators With Dr. Tina H. Boogren* (www.selfcarefor educators.com).

Timothy D. Kanold, PhD, is an award-winning educator and author. He is a former director of mathematics and science and served as superintendent of Adlai E. Stevenson High School District 125, the original Model Professional Learning Community (PLC) district in Lincolnshire, Illinois.

Dr. Kanold has authored or coauthored more than thirty textbooks and books on K–12 mathematics, school culture, and school leadership, including his bestselling and 2018 Independent Publisher Book Award-winning book *HEART! Fully Forming Your Professional Life as a Teacher and Leader*. In 2021 he authored a sequel to *HEART!*, the book *SOUL! Fulfilling the Promise of Your Professional Life as a Teacher and Leader*. He most recently coauthored with Tina H. Boogren the best-selling 2022 book *Educator Wellness: A Guide for Sustaining Physical, Mental, Emotional, and Social Well-Being*.

Dr. Kanold received the 2017 Ross Taylor / Glenn Gilbert National Leadership Award from the National Council of Supervisors of Mathematics, the international 2010 Damen Award for outstanding contributions to education from Loyola University Chicago, and the 1986 Presidential Award for Excellence in Mathematics and Science Teaching.

Dr. Kanold earned a bachelor's degree in education and a master's degree in applied mathematics from Illinois State University. He received his doctorate in educational leadership and counseling psychology from Loyola University Chicago.

Dr. Kanold is committed to equity, excellence, and social justice reform for the improved learning of students and school faculty, staff, and administrators. He conducts inspirational professional development seminars worldwide with a focus on improving student learning outcomes through a commitment to the PLC at Work process and a focus on living a well-balanced, fully engaged professional life by practicing reflection and self-care routines.

To learn more about Dr. Kanold's work, follow him @tkanold, #heartandsoul4ED, or #liveyourbestlife on Twitter.

Jasmine K. Kullar, EdD, is an assistant superintendent of a large metropolitan school district in Georgia. She is also a faculty member in the College of Professional Studies Educational Leadership Department at a postsecondary institution. Her experiences include working with the Wallace Foundation's University Principal Preparation Initiative (UPPI) and redesigning university educational leadership preparation programs.

Prior to these roles, she was a middle school principal for seven years at two separate schools. With over ten years of school leadership experience, Dr. Kullar has a variety of experience working at the elementary, middle, and high school levels in both Canada and the United States.

Dr. Kullar's experience with PLCs began in her first year of teaching over twenty years ago when she attended a PLC workshop and heard Dr. Richard DuFour and Dr. Robert Eaker speak. Since then, she has been implementing those tenets as a teacher. When she became a school administrator, she led her school to become the first in the state of Georgia to receive Model PLC status and garnered statewide attention for professional learning communities.

Dr. Kullar is the author of *Connecting Through Leadership: The Promise of Precise and Effective Communication in Schools*; coauthor of *Building Your Building: How to Hire and Keep Great Teachers*; and coeditor of *Women Who Lead: Insights, Inspiration, and Guidance to Grow as an Educator*. She has worked with schools and districts in more than twenty-five U.S. states. Her work includes keynoting, speaking, coaching teams, facilitating professional development for small and large groups, and working to develop school and district leadership teams. Her areas of expertise include PLCs, response to intervention, educator wellness, women in leadership, and building and supporting teacher leadership teams.

Dr. Kullar earned her undergraduate degree from the University of Toronto, her graduate degree from Memorial University of Newfoundland, and her doctorate from Argosy University in Atlanta. She has continued learning after her doctorate by participating in various programs and earning several certificates, including from Harvard's Leading Education Systems at the National Level program.

To book Tina H. Boogren, Timothy D. Kanold, or Jasmine K. Kullar for professional development, contact pd@SolutionTree.com.

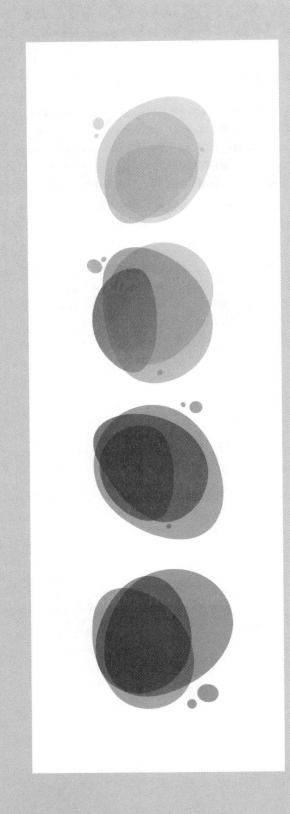

PART 1

ABOUT THIS PLAN BOOK AND JOURNAL

Great things are not done by impulse, but by a
series of small things brought together.

—Vincent Van Gogh

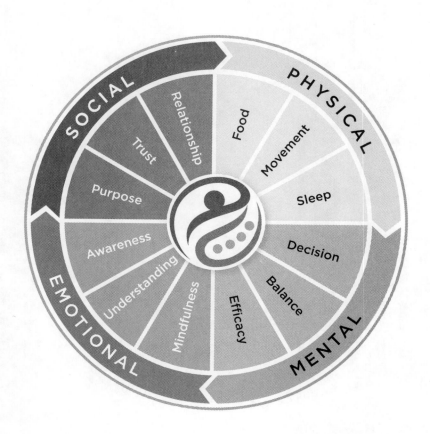

Welcome

We are excited that you have decided to use this plan book and journal, which is a companion to *Educator Wellness: A Guide for Sustaining Physical, Mental, Emotional, and Social Well-Being* (Kanold & Boogren, 2022). Typical of most school year planners, this resource provides space for your monthly and weekly calendar needs. This plan book and journal also offers the benefit of working on your own wellness throughout the school year. As a result, you will encounter weekly wellness *invitations* that will sustain you, your energy, and your positive disposition into summer, fall, winter, and spring.

As educators, we immerse ourselves daily in social experiences and our common humanity with others—including colleagues, students, and our community families. However, that immersion requires compassion, and compassion fatigue can affect our physical, mental, emotional, and social well-being.

Dates and deadlines arrive on our calendars. Sometimes we rush past them, but more deadlines and pressures loom. We plan, prepare, and do the best we can; then the next month or season arrives and before we know it, the school year has ended. It's over. We tuck away that year's planners and prepare for the next season of school and life ahead.

This plan book and journal's purpose is to serve and support your weekly planning while improving your wellness routines. We hope the journaling aspect of this plan book inspires or reinspires you to take back your joy and create more magical moments. We also remind you to cherish the people you work with and the people you love. Use this book to capture the busy details of your life and find the time each day to bring peace and kindness to yourself and those around you.

We believe your educator wellness is "a continuous, active process toward achieving a positive state of good health and enhanced physical, mental, emotional, and social well-being" (Kanold & Boogren, 2022, p. 1). May this book allow you to see, feel, and experience the wellness and well-being inside and around you as you engage in your important and meaningful work in this school year and this season of your life.

Tina H. Boogren

How to Use This Plan Book and Journal

An effective planning process helps reduce your load. Because every decision you make impacts your cognitive ability, using this book to effectively plan and journal will focus your decisions while helping to minimize daily stress through the benefit of weekly wellness reflections.

A good planner ideally supports the organizational load of remembering by providing space to record tasks, schedule events and meetings, and reflect. In addition, a well-crafted and intentional plan for each week creates a written record of accomplishments, a road map for future planning, and an opportunity to thrive in your everyday home and work life.

In this plan book and journal, you will find more than monthly and weekly calendars. Whole-life weekly invitations help you lead your personal wellness and well-being journey during the school year. A variety of tools are provided to support your responses to these invitations.

Educator Wellness Work

The graphic model (see figure P1.1, page 6) for the Wellness Solutions for Educators™ framework connects directly to this plan book and journal (Kanold & Boogren, 2022). There are twelve routines to consider as you reflect on your wellness plan progress, create meaningful and focused short-term and long-term professional wellness goals, and take action to achieve those goals. Beginning with June, and for each consecutive month, one of the twelve routines will be a primary focus for your wellness journey. The weekly planners invite you to focus on the specific routine assigned to each month. In addition, you will find frequent references to the Wellness Solutions for Educators™ framework that will support your growth as an educator and your impact on students and colleagues. As you use this plan book and journal, know that improving your routines in each wellness dimension can exponentially improve the quality of your work and life. The following sections discuss the planning elements that appear in each season, while the tools for support can be found in appendix A (page 227).

Source: Kanold & Boogren, 2022, p. 3.

Figure P1.1: Wellness Solutions for Educators framework graphic model.

Season-by-Season Planning and Wellness Work

As you begin planning, you will notice four sections labeled by season: summer, fall, winter, and spring. These sections present brief insight into the season (a three-month calendar cycle) and ask you to respond in advance to a few wellness questions for that season of your professional life. Those seasons and months are as follows.

- Summer: A Season of Renewal
  June, July, and August

- Fall: A Season of Opportunity
  September, October, and November

- Winter: A Season of Perseverance
  December, January, and February

- Spring: A Season of Transition
  March, April, and May

Each of the four seasons corresponds to the four dimensions of the Wellness Solutions for Educators framework: (1) physical, (2) mental, (3) emotional, and (4) social wellness—in that intentional order.

Your reflections and actions specific to physical wellness in the summer present great opportunities to build routines that will serve you well during the school year. Once the school year begins, actions and reflections built around your mental wellness help preserve your energy and enthusiasm as this part of your planning season unfolds. During the shorter hours of daylight and what can sometimes feel like the long slog of the winter months, sustaining your daily and weekly effort can be challenging. Therefore, you build upon your emotional wellness routines. Finally, spring arrives, and you can feel the end of the school year drawing near. During this season, focus on finishing well by working on your social wellness routines.

The *What's Next* sections at the end of each season offer transitioning advice followed by space for personal reflections as you prepare for the next three-month planning season.

Monthly Work and Calendar

Every month begins with a brief statement about that month's wellness focus, along with space to makes notes and answer questions about that month's routine. The monthly sections include a two-page calendar with space for planning notes at the beginning and throughout the month. This planner section provides plenty of space to use in any way you prefer. For example, you can record daily activities and appointments and use the notes section as needed. For the three summer month calendars, use them to plan forward, as you set instructional goals and actions for the following school year.

Weekly Planners, Invitations, and Reflections

Each month has five weekly planners since months begin and end on different days of the week. Each weekly planner includes the following sections.

- **Inspirational quote:** Take a moment to think about and connect to the quote and reflect on it throughout the week.

- **Invitation:** Wellness invitations focus on strategies for the specific wellness routine assigned to that month. Use these weekly invitations to take small steps forward on your wellness journey. Some of the invitations ask you to collect data or reflect on your wellness. In many cases, the invitations include supportive tools that can be found in appendix A (page 227).

- **Weekly planning calendar:** Each weekly calendar is a two-page spread with plenty of room for writing your plans and notes. Use this space as you would any other weekly calendar.

- **End-of-week reflection:** At the end of each week, you are asked to reflect on your wellness actions. Reflection helps you recognize your successful actions and challenges you to consider actions you might want to bring into the new week. You can use the prompts provided in the book or reflect on your own.

- **End-of-month reflection:** The end of each month provides a set of four wellness reflection questions connected to your wellness routine focus for that month. The questions ask you to reflect on:

- The weekly quotes and your responses to them
- Your wellness action celebrations and challenges
- A few *I will* wellness action commitments for the months ahead
- Additional thoughts about your progress

This book includes forty-six tools to support your wellness work, in appendix A (page 227). We present the tools by season and provide space to organize your thoughts, reflections, and data for many of the weekly wellness prompts. In addition, appendix B (page 277) offers resources to self-score your current progress for that month's specific wellness routine.

The Why

Whether you are a new or experienced educator, you are the sum of all the stories that make up your life, and you are the author of that story. Your planning, decisions, relationships, and sense of purpose all serve to create your personal story and path as an educator.

The work of this book centers around these questions: How do you bring your best self to your students and colleagues each day? How do you avoid the mental and emotional funk and exhaustion that waits in every school season? Which wellness habits and routines can have the most significant impact on your wellness and well-being as an educator, season after season?

Your wellness is a personal journey of self-reflection, habits, and routines for a lifetime of continuous improvement. Each year you build your path as an educator as you walk it. You plan, you act, you reflect, and plan again. The dates in your planner always arrive.

Your wellness journey will ebb and flow based on work and life circumstances. You will experience setbacks, and that's OK. The best wellness routines become sustainable when you start with small victories, view any setbacks as data and use those data as an invitation to keep moving forward—one step at a time. You have a wonderful wellness story to tell, and this plan book and journal can support and reveal your story and your history.

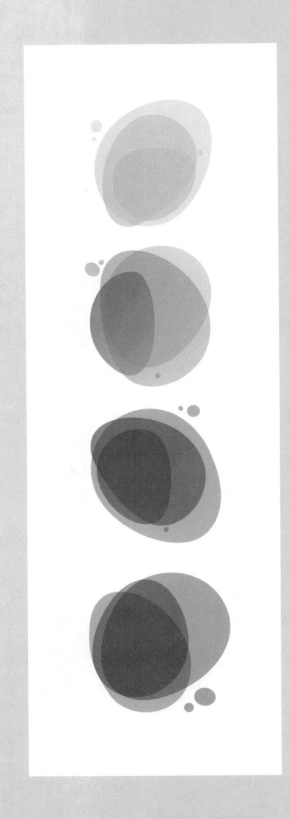

PART 2

SUMMER: A SEASON OF RENEWAL

I can shake off everything as I write; my sorrows
disappear, my courage is reborn.

—Anne Frank

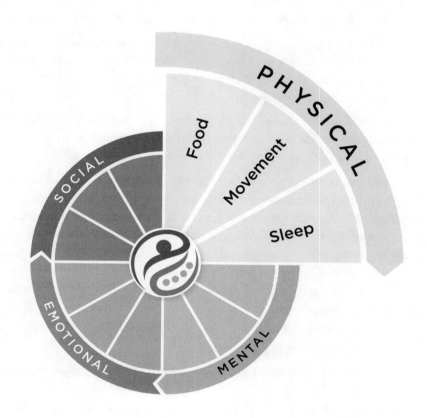

Summer Overview and Reflection: Physical Wellness

You begin summer with the dimension of *physical* wellness because when you feel better, you *are* better. When you properly hydrate and eat foods that provide healthy energy, you can move your body more. And when you move your body more, you typically sleep better (Rath, 2013). When you intentionally focus on these three areas of your daily life, you create a positive, interactive cycle of food, movement, and sleep routines.

The start of any new school year brings stress, no matter how many years you've been in the field. As you think about how you want to feel as you begin the next school year, you can use physical wellness routine improvements during the summer to help you develop habits and behaviors that will allow you to bring your best self to work each day.

By getting a jump start on your physical wellness routines during the summer, you'll set yourself up for success as you prepare for students to return to school. Use this time away from the daily grind of your professional life wisely.

The summer is a great time to focus on how well you take care of yourself *physically* as a first and primary wellness responsibility. You will gain a deeper understanding of the interconnections between the three wellness routines of food, movement, and sleep and how each routine deeply impacts your life inside and outside of school. You will thrive as an educator as you reflect on and improve your physical wellness routines. Your positive food, movement, and sleep actions help you to meet your most foundational needs head-on as you measure your preparation and progress for the new school season ahead. Each month focuses on the following routines.

- June's physical wellness routine is *food.* Consider what and when you eat and drink and how well you hydrate during the day.

- July's physical wellness routine is *movement.* Consider what, when, and how well you move each day.

- August's physical wellness routine is *sleep.* Consider how much sleep *and* daily rest you get during each twenty-four-hour cycle.

As you begin this season, reflect on and respond to the following prompts.

1. How does focusing on the physical wellness routines of food, movement, and sleep make you feel? Do you feel challenged, exhausted, excited, or maybe uncertain?

_____

_____

_____

_____

2. Reflect on your current personal and professional life. When has your body *felt* the best? What helped you feel so good? (Were you sleeping well? Committed to an exercise routine? Eating at home more often than out? Sharing time with a friend?)

_____

_____

_____

_____

3. What are your current celebrations and challenges around your daily physical wellness routines of food, movement, and sleep?

_____

_____

_____

_____

4. How important are the physical wellness routines of food, movement, and sleep to your closest family members, friends, and colleagues? How might you encourage others to support you or join you as you begin working on your physical wellness routines over the next three months?

_____

_____

_____

_____

5. Record any additional thoughts and reflections about your current physical wellness routines.

_____

_____

_____

_____

SUMMER

June

Monday	Tuesday	Wednesday

Focus: Food Routines
(Physical Wellness)

Thursday	Friday	Saturday	Sunday

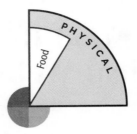

June: Food and Hydration Routines

The focus for June is on your *food and hydration* routines. Eating the proper food and staying hydrated with water is vital to your physical wellness. According to Harvard Health Publishing (2022), eating healthy helps you have more energy, avoid illness, and look and feel better. In addition, staying hydrated with water can flush toxins out of your system, help carry nutrients and oxygen to your cells, and ease digestion.

Since eating well is fundamental to your good health and overall well-being, in June, you will reflect on your current food choices and how the decisions about what you eat or drink make you feel as you strive for overall good nutrition (Newsom, 2023). What you eat and drink impacts your movement and sleep routines, which are the focus during July and August.

Each week in June, you are invited to experiment with one strategy for improving your food and hydration routines and actions. The weekly strategies for food and hydration follow.

Week One: Commit to making healthier food choices.

Week Two: Increase your water intake.

Week Three: Eat healthy meals throughout the day.

Week Four: Focus on eating without distractions.

Week Five: Monitor your food choices and the impact those choices have on your mood.

You can use the reflection and recording tools starting on page 18 as you move through each week's invitation. Before June begins, take time to pause for a brief food and hydration reflection and consider how your current food routines connect to how you feel each day.

Food and Hydration Notes and Reflections

Write about current celebrations or challenges regarding your food and hydration routines and describe how those routines impact your energy each week.

_____

_____

_____

_____

_____

_____

_____

_____

_____

_____

_____

_____

_____

_____

_____

_____

_____

_____

_____

_____

_____

_____

_____

_____

_____

_____

_____

_____

_____

_____

_____

_____

_____

_____

_____

_____

_____

_____

Week One:
Commit to Healthier Food Choices

Invitation: Clean out your pantry and refrigerator (for example, eliminate cookies, candy, chocolate, chips, and sugary drinks) to minimize access to unhealthy foods and drinks. Replace those foods with healthier ones, which will help you make healthier food choices. You can use the "Healthy Snacks List" tool (page 230) if needed.

Monday

Tuesday

Wednesday

If you keep good food in your fridge, you will eat good food.

—Errick McAdams

Thursday

Friday

Saturday

Sunday

End-of-Week Wellness Reflections

My celebrations:

_____

_____

_____

_____

My challenges:

_____

_____

_____

_____

_____

_____

My considerations for next week:

_____

_____

_____

_____

_____

_____

_____

Week Two:
Increase Your Water Intake

Invitation: Increase your water intake by selecting a water bottle and deciding when to drink more water (when first waking up, before a meal, and so on). Next, associate a habit with drinking water (every time you text or check the time). Finally, aim to drink about four to six cups of water each day (Harvard Health Publishing, 2022). You can use the "Water Tracker" tool (page 231) if needed.

Monday

Tuesday

Wednesday

Drinking water is like washing out your insides. The water will cleanse the system, fill you up, decrease your caloric load and improve the function of all your tissues.

—**Kevin R. Stone**

Thursday

Friday

Saturday

Sunday

End-of-Week Wellness Reflections

My celebrations:
_____
_____
_____
_____
_____
_____
_____
_____
_____

My challenges:
_____
_____
_____
_____
_____
_____
_____
_____

My considerations for next week:
_____
_____
_____
_____
_____
_____
_____
_____
_____
_____

Week Three:
Commit to Eating Healthy Meals

Invitation: Commit to eating healthy meals consisting of lean proteins and a variety of colorful vegetables and fruits throughout each day this week. You can use the "Healthy Meals Planner" tool (page 232) if needed.

Monday

Tuesday

Wednesday

Health requires healthy food.

Roger Williams

Thursday

Friday

Saturday

Sunday

End-of-Week Wellness Reflections

My celebrations:

_____
_____
_____
_____
_____
_____
_____
_____
_____

My challenges:

_____
_____
_____
_____
_____
_____
_____
_____

My considerations for next week:

_____
_____
_____
_____
_____
_____
_____
_____

Week Four:
Focus on Eating Without Distractions

Invitation: When eating, focus only on eating. Eliminate distractions while you eat, such as watching TV, answering emails and texts on your phone, driving in your car, or being on your computer.

Monday

Tuesday

Wednesday

The first wealth is health.

—Unknown

End-of-Week Wellness Reflections

My celebrations:

_____
_____
_____
_____

_____
_____
_____
_____

Thursday

My challenges:

_____
_____
_____
_____

Friday

_____
_____

My considerations for next week:

Saturday

Sunday

_____
_____
_____
_____
_____
_____

Week Five:
Monitor Food's Effect on Mood

Invitation: Monitor the food choices you make and the impact those choices have on your mood this week. For example, do your food choices make you feel more or less energetic? You can use the "Food Choice and Impact on Mood" tool (page 233) if needed.

Monday

Tuesday

Wednesday

To eat is a necessity, but to eat intelligently is an art.

— François de La Rochefoucauld

Thursday

Friday

Saturday

Sunday

End-of-Week Wellness Reflections

My celebrations:

_____
_____
_____
_____

_____
_____
_____
_____
_____

My challenges:

_____
_____
_____
_____
_____
_____
_____

My considerations for next week:

_____
_____
_____
_____
_____
_____
_____
_____
_____

End-of-Month Reflection: Food and Hydration Routines

As June ends, pause for a wellness reflection and respond to the following prompts.

1. Reread the five weekly food and hydration quotes from this month. Which quote resonated most for you? Why?

_____

_____

_____

_____

2. What did you learn about your own food and hydration routines this month? What were your celebrations? What were your challenges?

_____

_____

_____

_____

3. Write two *I will* actions regarding your food and hydration routines to carry over into July and August.

    a. I will:

_____

_____

_____

_____

    b. I will:

_____

_____

_____

_____

4. Record any additional thoughts and reflections about your progress this month.

_____

_____

_____

_____

For additional reflection on your food routine progress, go to appendix B (page 277) to self-score your current effort and actions.

Notes

_____

_____

_____

_____

_____

_____

_____

_____

_____

_____

_____

_____

_____

_____

_____

_____

_____

_____

_____

_____

_____

_____

_____

_____

_____

_____

_____

_____

_____

_____

_____

_____

_____

July

Monday	Tuesday	Wednesday

Focus: Movement Routines (Physical Wellness)

Thursday	Friday	Saturday	Sunday

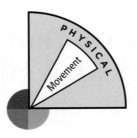

July: Movement Routines

The focus for July is on your daily *movement* routines. Scientific evidence points to the following incredible benefits of commitment to movement: enhanced learning, greater productivity, increased resilience to stress, improved mood, and slowed aging (Langshur & Klemp, 2016). Remember, movement includes the *what, when,* and *how* you move your body, such as how many steps you take throughout the day and how long you are on your feet as you avoid long periods of sitting.

Moving our bodies increases our energy levels—an essential ingredient for highly effective educators. You can use summer to focus on incremental movement actions that will help maximize and uplift your energy into the new school year.

Each week in July, you are invited to experiment with one strategy for improving your *movement* routines and actions. The weekly strategies for movement follow.

Week One: Track your sitting time during the day.

Week Two: Find time for your favorite movement activity.

Week Three: Set a goal of moving for 150 minutes throughout the week and track your progress toward the goal each day.

Week Four: Ask a partner to join you for a 70,000 steps-in-a-week challenge.

Week Five: Be intentional about placing movement activities into your calendar.

You can use the reflection and recording tools starting on page 34 as you move through each week's invitation. Before July begins, take time to pause for a brief movement reflection and consider how your current movement routines connect to how you feel each day.

Movement Notes and Reflections

Write about current celebrations or challenges regarding your movement routines and describe how those routines impact your energy each week.

_____

_____

_____

_____

Week One:
Track Your Sitting Time

Invitation: Track how much time you spend sitting during the day, how it impacts your mood, and how you feel at the end of the day. For example, consider the time spent in the car, sitting at the kitchen table, watching TV, working on your computer, at a live event, or at a restaurant. You can use the "Time Spent Sitting and Impact on Mood" tool (page 234) if needed.

Monday

Tuesday

Wednesday

Reducing the amount of time spent sitting down is more essential than brief, but vigorous exercise.

—Kelly McGonigal

Thursday

Friday

Saturday

Sunday

End-of-Week Wellness Reflections

My celebrations:

_____
_____
_____
_____
_____
_____
_____
_____
_____
_____

My challenges:

_____
_____
_____
_____
_____
_____
_____
_____
_____
_____

My considerations for next week:

_____
_____
_____
_____
_____
_____
_____
_____
_____
_____

Week Two:
Find Time for Your Favorite Movement Activity

Invitation: Ask yourself how your favorite movement activity makes you feel and decide how to fit the activity into your day. Remember, everything counts, including walking your dog, dancing, gardening, running, swimming, riding a bike, practicing yoga, and more. You can use the "List of Movement Activities" tool (page 235) if needed.

Monday

Tuesday

Wednesday

> To me, if life boils down to one thing, it's movement. To live is to keep moving.
>
> —Jerry Seinfeld

Thursday

Friday

Saturday

Sunday

End-of-Week Wellness Reflections

My celebrations:

_____
_____
_____
_____
_____
_____
_____
_____
_____

My challenges:

_____
_____
_____
_____
_____
_____
_____
_____
_____

My considerations for next week:

_____
_____
_____
_____
_____
_____
_____
_____
_____

Week Three:
Move 150 Minutes This Week

Invitation: Set a goal of moving 150 minutes during the week. Track how you do each day. Remember, you do not need to do 150 minutes of movement activity at once. You could do thirty minutes a day for five days. You can use the "Movement Minutes Tracker" tool (page 236) if needed.

Monday

Tuesday

Wednesday

Movement is the song of the body.

—Vanda Scaravelli

Thursday

Friday

Saturday

Sunday

End-of-Week Wellness Reflections

My celebrations:

_____
_____
_____
_____
_____
_____
_____
_____

My challenges:

_____
_____
_____
_____
_____
_____
_____
_____

My considerations for next week:

_____
_____
_____
_____
_____
_____
_____
_____
_____
_____

Week Four:
Find a Partner for the 70,000 Steps Challenge

Invitation: Ask a partner to join you for a 70,000 steps-in-a-week challenge within the next seven days. Support your movement goals together. Log your steps and then share, celebrate, and enjoy your success as a team wellness goal! Remember, all types of movement and steps count. One week, *together*. You can use the "70,000 Steps Challenge" tool (page 237) if needed.

Monday

Tuesday

Wednesday

Fight for the things you care about but do it in a way that will lead others to join you.

—Ruth Bader Ginsburg

Thursday

Friday

Saturday

Sunday

End-of-Week Wellness Reflections

My celebrations:

_____

_____

_____

_____

_____

_____

_____

_____

My challenges:

_____

_____

_____

_____

_____

_____

_____

My considerations
for next week:

_____

_____

_____

_____

_____

_____

_____

_____

Week Five:
Schedule Movement Activities

Invitation: Be intentional about scheduling movement activities each day. Indicate specific times, activities, and desired intensity levels. Remember, the movement activities you choose are not for comparison with others, but rather for your personal movement journey. You can use the "Movement Activity Tracker" tool (page 238) if needed.

Monday

Tuesday

Wednesday

Don't compare yourself to others. You have no idea what their journey is all about.

—Regina Brett

Thursday

Friday

Saturday

Sunday

End-of-Week Wellness Reflections

My celebrations:

_____
_____
_____
_____

_____
_____
_____
_____
_____

My challenges:

_____
_____
_____
_____
_____
_____
_____
_____

My considerations for next week:

_____
_____
_____
_____
_____
_____
_____

End-of-Month Reflection: Movement Routines

As July ends, pause for a wellness reflection and respond to the following prompts.

1. Reread the five weekly movement quotes from this month. Which quote resonated most for you? Why?

_____

_____

_____

_____

2. What did you learn about your own movement routines this month? What were your celebrations? What were your challenges?

_____

_____

_____

_____

3. Write two *I will* actions regarding your movement routines to carry over into August.

_____

_____

_____

_____

   a. I will:

_____

_____

_____

_____

   b. I will:

_____

_____

_____

_____

4. Record any additional thoughts and reflections about your movement progress this month and how it impacted your food routines from June.

_____

_____

_____

_____

For additional reflection on your movement routine progress, go to appendix B (page 277) to self-score your current effort and actions.

Notes

_____

_____

_____

_____

_____

_____

_____

_____

_____

_____

_____

_____

_____

_____

_____

_____

_____

_____

_____

_____

_____

_____

_____

_____

SUMMER

July

August

Monday	Tuesday	Wednesday

Focus: Sleep Routines (Physical Wellness)

Thursday	Friday	Saturday	Sunday

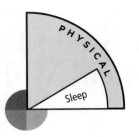

August: Sleep and Rest Routines

The focus for August is on your sleep *and* rest routines. How you feel as you begin the new school year largely depends on what happens when you sleep. Nothing works properly when you don't get enough sleep. Therefore, sleep acts as the cornerstone of your physical wellness routines. Consider how prioritizing your sleep during this school year will support the food and movement routine actions of the past two months. When you get enough sleep and incorporate brain break rest into your day, you are more likely to make food and movement choices that support your overall health and well-being.

Each week in August, you are invited to experiment with one strategy for improving your sleep routines. The weekly strategies for sleep follow.

Week One: Track how much time you spend sleeping each night.

Week Two: Create and implement a wind-down routine before bed.

Week Three: Incorporate one or two new recommended sleep strategies.

Week Four: Track how much rest time you take throughout your day.

Week Five: Incorporate purposeful rest into your day.

You can use the reflection and recording tools starting on page 50 as you move through each week's invitation. Before August begins, take time to pause for a brief sleep assessment by reflecting on how many hours of sleep you get each night, how well you fall asleep and stay asleep, whether you have breathing or snoring problems, and if you feel rested or have back or other pain after sleeping. Also consider how your current sleep routines are impacted by your food and movement routines.

Sleep and Rest Notes and Reflections

Write about current celebrations or challenges regarding sleep and rest routines and describe how those routines impact your energy each week.

_____

_____

_____

_____

_____

Week One:
Track How Much You Sleep

Invitation: Track how many hours of sleep you get each night. Also, note how you feel the following day. For example, do you feel energized? Sleepy? Grouchy? Happy? You can use the "Sleep Tracker" tool (page 239) if needed.

Monday

Tuesday

Wednesday

The best bridge between despair and hope is a good night's sleep.

—E. Joseph Cossman

Thursday

Friday

Saturday

Sunday

End-of-Week Wellness Reflections

My celebrations:

_____
_____
_____
_____

_____
_____
_____
_____
_____

My challenges:

_____
_____
_____
_____
_____
_____
_____

My considerations for next week:

_____
_____
_____
_____
_____
_____
_____
_____
_____

Week Two:
Create a Wind-Down Routine

Invitation: Create and implement a daily wind-down routine this week. This might include strategies such as turning off all electronics at a certain time, taking a bath, journaling, reading, or drinking a cup of decaffeinated tea. You can use the "Wind-Down Routine" tool (page 240) if needed.

Monday

_____

Tuesday

_____

Wednesday

Anything seems possible at night when the rest of the world has gone to sleep.

—David Almond

Thursday

Friday

Saturday

Sunday

End-of-Week Wellness Reflections

My celebrations:

_____
_____
_____
_____
_____
_____
_____

My challenges:

_____
_____
_____
_____
_____
_____
_____

My considerations
for next week:

_____
_____
_____
_____
_____
_____
_____

Week Three:
Incorporate Sleep Strategies

Invitation: Incorporate one or two new recommended sleep strategies this week. Suggested strategies include keeping your room cool and dark; going to bed at the same time each night; removing electronics from the bedroom; avoiding large meals, caffeine, and alcohol before bedtime; and keeping up with your movement routines from July.

Monday

Tuesday

Wednesday

Happiness is waking up, looking at the clock and finding that you still have two hours left to sleep.

—Charles M. Schulz

End-of-Week Wellness Reflections

My celebrations:
_____
_____
_____
_____
_____
_____
_____
_____

Thursday

My challenges:
_____
_____
_____
_____
_____
_____
_____
_____

Friday

My considerations
for next week:
_____
_____
_____
_____
_____
_____
_____
_____

Saturday

Sunday

Week Four:
Track Rest Time

Invitation: Track how much rest time you get throughout your days this week. *Rest* means taking a small break during the workday. Consider what rest looks and feels like on days you can rest versus days you're unable to rest or can't rest for very long. You can use the "Rest-Time Tracker" tool (page 241) if needed.

Monday

Tuesday

Wednesday

When the going gets tough, the tough take a nap.

—Tom Hodgkinson

End-of-Week Wellness Reflections

My celebrations:

_____
_____
_____
_____
_____
_____
_____
_____
_____

Thursday

My challenges:

_____
_____
_____
_____
_____
_____
_____

Friday

My considerations
for next week:

_____
_____
_____
_____
_____
_____
_____
_____

Saturday

Sunday

Week Five:
Incorporate Purposeful Rest

Invitation: Incorporate purposeful rest into your days this week. Purposeful rest is any stress-reducing activity, such as going for a quick walk, doing a mindfulness meditation, or simply pausing for some deep breaths while looking away from the computer screen.

Monday

Tuesday

Wednesday

A well-spent day brings happy sleep.

— **Leonardo da Vinci**

End-of-Week Wellness Reflections

My celebrations:

_____
_____
_____
_____
_____
_____
_____
_____

Thursday

My challenges:

_____
_____
_____
_____
_____
_____
_____
_____
_____

Friday

My considerations
for next week:

_____
_____
_____

Saturday | **Sunday**

_____
_____
_____
_____
_____
_____
_____

End-of-Month Reflection: Sleep and Rest Routines

As August ends, pause for a wellness reflection and respond to the following prompts.

1. Reread the five weekly sleep and rest quotes from this month. Which quote resonated most for you? Why?

_____
_____
_____
_____

2. What did you learn about your own sleep and rest routines this month? What were your celebrations? What were your challenges?

_____
_____
_____
_____

3. Write two *I will* actions regarding your sleep and rest routines to carry over into September.

   a. I will:

_____
_____
_____
_____

   b. I will:

_____
_____
_____
_____

4. Record any additional thoughts and reflections about your progress this month and for the past three months as the summer ends. How do you feel? How do the three physical wellness routines of food, movement, and sleep interconnect for you? What did you notice about how one routine impacts the others?

_____

_____

_____

_____

For additional reflection on your sleep and rest routine progress, go to appendix B (page 277) to self-score your current effort and actions.

Notes

_____

_____

_____

_____

_____

_____

_____

_____

_____

_____

_____

_____

_____

_____

_____

_____

_____

_____

_____

_____

_____

_____

_____

_____

_____

End of Summer: What's Next?

Remember to be patient with yourself. Small tweaks and minor changes in your food, movement, and sleep routines can quickly add up to produce a better you. You don't have to change it all in one day; in fact, you can't change it all in one day. You simply need to start, and that's what you did during June, July, and August as you prepared for the new school season ahead.

Of course, you will experience setbacks, and that's OK. The best routines become sustainable when you start with small victories, create greater awareness and understanding of your physical wellness routines, and then set short-term and long-term goals for improvement. View any setbacks as data and use those data as an invitation to keep moving forward, one step at a time.

As you focus on your physical wellness routines, take time to reflect on how improvements in these three routines impact how you feel each day. Then you can use Labor Day weekend to celebrate your physical wellness progress and set some new goals for fall.

During the next season, your focus will be on the *mental wellness* dimension of daily life. According to the World Health Organization (2018), your mental wellness is a "state of well-being in which the individual realizes his or her own abilities, can cope with the normal stresses of life, can work productively and fruitfully, and is able to make a contribution to his or her community."

September, October, and November present a *Season of Opportunity* as you settle into the new school year. You will explore the daily wellness routines of *decision, balance,* and *efficacy* and how these mental wellness routines also support your food, movement, and sleep goals from the summer.

Ready? Let's go!

Notes

_____

_____

_____

_____

_____

_____

_____

_____

_____

_____

_____

_____

_____

_____

_____

_____

_____

_____

_____

_____

_____

_____

_____

_____

_____

_____

_____

_____

_____

_____

_____

_____

_____

_____

_____

_____

_____

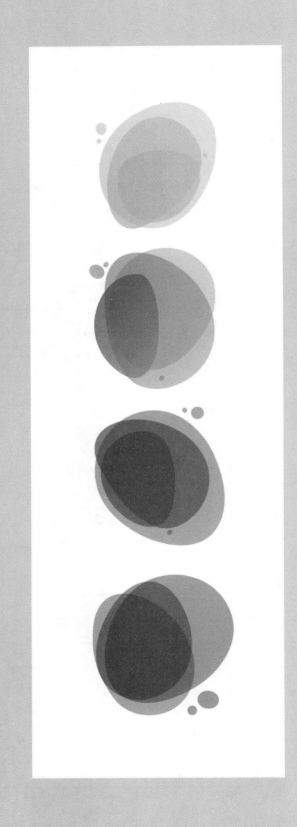

PART 3

FALL: A SEASON OF OPPORTUNITY

When you feel mentally well, you work more
productively, enjoy free time more, contribute more
actively in your community, and are more likely to
practice routines of self-care and kindness.

—Mental Health Foundation

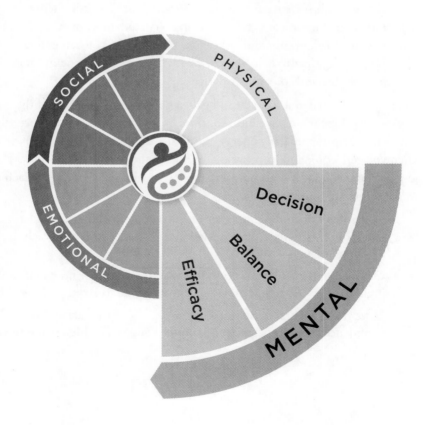

Fall Overview and Reflection: Mental Wellness

You begin fall with the dimension of *mental* wellness because this season is a great time to focus on thriving mentally as you settle into the rhythm, challenges, and benefits of a new school year. During September, your busy and highly engaged work and home life ramp up. Stress levels begin to rise. Being busy can be beneficial stress when you are able to anticipate and act on everything you want to accomplish during the school year. However, if you are not careful this stress can cross over into a daily, hurried, out-of-control, prolonged-stress work life.

Fall is the season to think of mental wellness as a state of well-being in which you successfully cope with the stressors of life and realize your work-life self-efficacy, which is the belief and confidence in your ability to help every student learn every day as you create and share new knowledge with your colleagues. Thankfully, you can embrace preemptive and self-regulatory routines to help you cope with the stress, high energy, unexpected adversity, and relentless demands of your work life.

For the next three months, you will gain a deeper understanding of the interconnections between the three mental wellness routines of decision-making, balance, and self-efficacy, and how these support daily energy and positive presence. You will thrive as an educator when you reflect on and improve these three mental wellness routines. They will sustain you and help you meet your most essential work and life challenges. Each month focuses on the following routines.

- September's mental wellness routine is *decision*-making. Consider how well you reduce, automate, and regulate the decisions you make each day to avoid decision fatigue.

- October's mental wellness routine is *balance*. Consider how well you live a busy, high-energy, well-balanced day-to-day work life to avoid prolonged stress.

- November's mental wellness routine is *self-efficacy*. Consider how well you build confidence and competence and improve your work-life capabilities daily.

As you begin the season, reflect on and respond to the following prompts.

1. How does focusing on the mental wellness routines of decision, balance, and efficacy make you feel? Do you feel challenged, exhausted, excited, or maybe uncertain?

_____

_____

_____

_____

2. Identify a time in your professional life when you were thriving at work. What helped you to mentally feel so good?

_____

_____

_____

_____

3. What are your current celebrations and challenges around your daily mental wellness routines of decision-making, balance, and self-efficacy?

_____

_____

_____

_____

4. How important are the mental wellness routines of decision-making, balance, and self-efficacy to your closest family members, friends, and colleagues? How might you encourage others to support you or join you as you begin working on your mental wellness routines over the next three months?

_____

_____

_____

_____

5. Record any other thoughts and reflections about your current mental wellness routines.

_____

_____

_____

_____

FALL

September

Sept.

FALL

Monday	Tuesday	Wednesday

Focus: Decision Routines (Mental Wellness)

Thursday	Friday	Saturday	Sunday

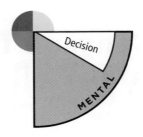

September: Decision Routines

The focus for September is on your *decision* (or decision-making) routines. Your professional responsibilities call on you to make many difficult (and wise) decisions. The sheer volume of those decisions can be exhausting when you learn that educators make 1,500 educational decisions daily at work and over 35,000 general decisions for the entire day (Goldberg & Houser, 2017). The consequences of all these decisions are real. As the day wears on, your decision-making wisdom wears down, decision fatigue sets in, and your brain seeks shortcuts. At this point, you either make decisions impulsively or avoid decision making altogether, which are concerning for your daily well-being. Therefore, your focus this month is on tackling decision fatigue.

By becoming intentional about your daily decision-making routines, you strengthen your mental wellness. Additionally, you can use the strategies you build this month to strengthen your physical wellness routines.

Each week in September, you are invited to experiment with one strategy for improving your decision-making routines. The weekly strategies for decision follow.

Week One: Track how many decisions you make during the school day.

Week Two: Create daily habits and routines that reduce your number of decisions.

Week Three: Establish firm boundaries around your time at work.

Week Four: Schedule fifteen minutes per day just for you.

Week Five: Develop your self-compassion through daily affirmations.

You can use the reflection and recording tools starting on page 72 as you move through each week's invitation. Before September begins, take time to pause for a brief decision-making reflection.

Decision Notes and Reflections

Write about current celebrations or challenges regarding your decision-making routines and describe how those routines impact your energy and mental fatigue each week.

_____

_____

_____

Week One:
Track Decisions

Invitation: Track how many decisions you make during the school day. You can keep a tally on scratch paper or use the "Decision Tracker" tool (page 242) if needed.

Sept.

FALL

Monday

Tuesday

Wednesday

We all make choices, but in the end, our choices make us.

— Ken Levine

Thursday

Friday

Saturday

Sunday

End-of-Week Wellness Reflections

My celebrations:

_____
_____
_____
_____
_____
_____
_____

My challenges:

_____
_____
_____
_____
_____
_____

My considerations for next week:

_____
_____
_____
_____
_____
_____
_____
_____

FALL

Sept.

Week Two:
Create Daily Habits

Invitation: Create daily habits and routines to reduce your number of daily decisions. For example, create a ritual around preparing for the next day, respond to emails, return calls or text messages at a designated time, or grade papers and design lessons at the same time each day. You can use the "Daily Habit and Routine Commitments" tool (page 243) if needed.

Monday

Tuesday

Wednesday

Once you make a decision, the universe conspires to make it happen.

—Ralph Waldo Emerson

Thursday

Friday

Saturday

Sunday

End-of-Week Wellness Reflections

My celebrations:

_____
_____
_____
_____
_____
_____
_____
_____

My challenges:

_____
_____
_____
_____
_____
_____
_____

My considerations for next week:

_____
_____
_____
_____
_____
_____
_____
_____
_____

FALL

Sept.

Week Three:
Establish Boundaries Around Worktime

Invitation: Establish firm boundaries around your time at work this week. Examples include sticking to planned agendas for meetings, creating expectations for shared duties with colleagues, and honoring team meeting norms.

Sept.

FALL

Monday

Tuesday

Wednesday

A good decision is based on knowledge and not on numbers.

— Plato

Thursday

Friday

Saturday

Sunday

End-of-Week Wellness Reflections

My celebrations:

_____
_____
_____
_____
_____
_____
_____
_____
_____

My challenges:

_____
_____
_____
_____
_____
_____
_____

My considerations for next week:

_____
_____
_____
_____
_____
_____
_____
_____
_____

Week Four:
Schedule Time for You

Invitation: Schedule fifteen minutes per day that are just for you. Include this time in your calendar like any other appointment and engage in self-care, such as physical movement, reading, journaling, practicing yoga, sitting in silence, gardening, or listening to a podcast. You can use the "Brainstorm Activities That Are Just for You" tool (page 244) if needed.

FALL

Sept.

Monday

Tuesday

Wednesday

> There is no decision that we can make that doesn't come with some sort of balance or sacrifice.
>
> —Simon Sinek

Thursday

Friday

Saturday

Sunday

End-of-Week Wellness Reflections

My celebrations:

_____
_____
_____

_____
_____
_____
_____
_____
_____

My challenges:

_____
_____
_____

_____
_____
_____
_____

My considerations for next week:

_____
_____
_____
_____
_____
_____
_____
_____
_____
_____

FALL

Sept.

Week Five:
Develop Self-Compassion

Invitation: Develop self-compassion through daily affirmations. Create your own affirmations or use these: (1) I treat myself with kindness, (2) I forgive myself when I make mistakes, (3) I am learning every day, (4) I am doing my best, (5) I love myself, (6) It's OK for me to not be perfect, and (7) I am powerful and strong. You can use the "Your Daily Affirmations" tool (page 245) if needed.

Sept.

FALL

Monday

Tuesday

Wednesday

Keep your temper. A decision made in anger is never sound.

—Ford Frick

Thursday

Friday

Saturday

Sunday

End-of-Week Wellness Reflections

My celebrations:

_____
_____
_____
_____
_____
_____
_____
_____

My challenges:

_____
_____
_____
_____
_____
_____
_____
_____

My considerations for next week:

_____
_____
_____
_____
_____
_____
_____
_____

FALL

Sept.

End-of-Month Reflection: Decision Routines

As September ends, pause for a wellness reflection and respond to the following prompts.

1. Reread the five weekly decision quotes from this month. Which quote resonated most for you? Why?

_____

_____

_____

_____

2. What did you learn about your decision-making routines this month? What were your celebrations? What were your challenges?

_____

_____

_____

_____

3. Write two *I will* actions regarding your decision-making routines to carry over into October and November.

   a. I will:

   _____

   _____

   _____

   _____

   b. I will:

   _____

   _____

   _____

   _____

4. Record any additional thoughts and reflections about your decision-making progress this month and how it impacted your physical wellness routines from the summer.

_____

_____

_____

_____

For additional reflection on your decision-making routine progress, go to appendix B (page 277) to self-score your current effort and actions.

Notes

October

F A L L

Oct.

Monday	Tuesday	Wednesday

Focus: Balance Routines
(Mental Wellness)

Thursday	Friday	Saturday	Sunday

FALL

Oct.

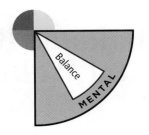

October: Balance Routines

The focus for October is on your *balance* routines because every day at work requires high positive energy. The relational energy it takes to meet the daily expectations of your students and colleagues can be exhausting. Most days bring a surprise, challenge, or nuance that needs your time and attention. You are busy, which can feel great until you cross that fine line between a full, busy life and an out-of-control, *hurried* life.

It is possible to sustain an improved and constant high-energy state at work and home. However, to do so requires your brain be given time to rest and recover from the noise of each day. Internal balance requires time for daily silence and solitude. Sherry Turkle (2012), founding director of the MIT Initiative on Technology and Self, verifies that the door to successful relationships is purposeful solitude, with an embraced silence, especially regarding our technologies.

Each week in October, you are invited to experiment with one strategy for improving your daily balance routines and actions. The weekly strategies for balance follow.

Week One: Track your daily activities. Are you busy or hurried?

Week Two: Track your energy during the day. Is it high or low, positive, or negative?

Week Three: Track your verbal communications with others.

Week Four: Commit to taking time to eliminate all inputs and noise.

Week Five: Ask several colleagues and family members for feedback.

You can use the reflection and recording tools starting on page 88 as you move through each week's invitation. Before October begins, take time to pause for a brief balance routine reflection and consider how your current routines connect to how you feel each day.

Balance Notes and Reflections

Write about current celebrations or challenges regarding your balance routines and describe how those routines impact your energy each week.

_____

_____

_____

_____

Week One:
Track Daily Activities

Invitation: Track how your daily activities make you feel either *busy* (thriving, fully present, in-demand, satisfied, and loving the action) or *hurried* (anxious, unable to be fully present with others, not enough time, physically and emotionally exhausted). You can use the "Busy or Hurried Tracker" tool (page 246) if needed.

FALL

Oct.

Monday

Tuesday

Wednesday

You must ruthlessly eliminate hurry from your life.

—Dallas Willard

Thursday

Friday

Saturday

Sunday

End-of-Week Wellness Reflections

My celebrations:

_____
_____
_____
_____
_____
_____
_____
_____

My challenges:

_____
_____
_____
_____
_____
_____
_____

My considerations for next week:

_____
_____
_____
_____
_____
_____
_____

FALL

Oct.

Week Two:
Track Your Energy

Invitation: This week, keep track of the your overall positive energy state throughout the day and evening. In a high-positive energy state you are feeling hopeful, helpful, confident, joyful, and connected. In a low-positive energy state you are relaxed, reflective, serene, tranquil, peaceful, and quiet. You can use the "Positive Energy State Tracker" tool (page 247) if needed.

FALL
Oct.

Monday

Tuesday

Wednesday

Energy and persistence conquer all things.

—Benjamin Franklin

Thursday

Friday

Saturday

Sunday

End-of-Week Wellness Reflections

My celebrations:

_____
_____
_____
_____
_____
_____
_____
_____

My challenges:

_____
_____
_____
_____
_____
_____

My considerations for next week:

_____
_____
_____
_____
_____
_____
_____

FALL

Oct.

Week Three:
Track Verbal Communications

Invitation: Track your verbal communications. Do your words reflect negativity, such as in the form of blaming, judging, or overgeneralizing ("*all* of my students don't care")? Do your words reflect positivity, such as listening to others, celebrating their ideas, and respectfully talking about students? You can use the "Verbal Communications Tracker" tool (page 248) if needed.

Monday

Tuesday

Wednesday

I have never, ever focused on the negative of things. I always look at the positive.

—Sonia Sotomayor

Thursday

Friday

Saturday

Sunday

End-of-Week Wellness Reflections

My celebrations:
_____
_____
_____
_____
_____
_____
_____

My challenges:
_____
_____
_____
_____

My considerations for next week:
_____
_____
_____
_____
_____
_____
_____

FALL

Oct.

Week Four:
Eliminate Inputs and Noise

Invitation: Make time to eliminate all inputs and noise (including technologies) from your daily life and sit in solitude and silence for at least fifteen minutes *each day*. Be intentional about making time for this by marking it on your calendar. Reflect on how you feel during this time. You can use the "Eliminate Inputs and Noise Tracker" tool (page 249) if needed.

FALL

Oct.

Monday

Tuesday

Wednesday

> I fear that moments of quietude are on the endangered list; right behind solitude.
>
> —Nanette L. Avery

Thursday

Friday

Saturday

Sunday

End-of-Week Wellness Reflections

My celebrations:

_____
_____
_____
_____
_____
_____
_____
_____

My challenges:

_____
_____
_____
_____
_____
_____

My considerations for next week:

_____
_____
_____
_____
_____
_____
_____

FALL · Oct.

Week Five:
Ask for Feedback

Invitation: Ask several colleagues and family members whether you demonstrate a high-energy, well-balanced, professional, and joyful self—a life where you are confident, connected, hopeful, and happy—on most days. Record their responses. You can use the "Record of Feedback" tool (page 250) if needed.

FALL

Oct.

Monday

Tuesday

Wednesday

Be yourself. Everyone else is taken.

—Menards advertisement

Thursday

Friday

Saturday

Sunday

End-of-Week Wellness Reflections

My celebrations:
_____
_____
_____
_____
_____
_____
_____
_____

My challenges:
_____
_____
_____
_____
_____
_____
_____
_____
_____

My considerations for next week:
_____
_____
_____
_____
_____
_____
_____
_____
_____

End-of-Month Reflection: Balance Routines

As October ends, pause for a wellness reflection and respond to the following prompts.

1. Reread the five weekly balance quotes from this month. Which quote resonated most for you? Why?

_____

_____

_____

_____

2. What did you learn about your personal balance routines this month? What were your celebrations? What were your challenges?

_____

_____

_____

_____

3. Write two *I will* actions regarding your balance routines to carry over into November.

   a. I will:

   _____

   _____

   _____

   _____

   b. I will:

   _____

   _____

   _____

   _____

4. Record any additional thoughts and reflections about your balance routines progress this month and how it may have improved your decision-making routines.

_____

_____

_____

_____

For additional reflection on your balance routine progress, go to appendix B (page 277) to self-score your current effort and actions.

Notes

November

Monday	Tuesday	Wednesday

Focus: Efficiency Routines (Mental Wellness)

Thursday	Friday	Saturday	Sunday

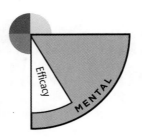

November: Efficacy Routines

The focus for November is on your *efficacy* (or *self-efficacy*) routines because you are more productive when you practice self-care and kindness. *Efficacy* refers to what you believe to be true about *your* capabilities—your competence and confidence to meet the expectations of your work and home life. Strengthening competence and confidence is hard work because past experiences can shape your beliefs about your knowledge, skills, and abilities.

Because life experiences are continuous, strengthening your confidence is a lifelong journey. Investing time to build confidence is a primary distinguishing factor of successful people. By possessing strong self-confidence, you're more likely to be happy, willing to change, have better relationships, and more (Bandura, 2012).

Each week in November, you are invited to experiment with one strategy for improving your daily efficacy routines and actions to build a more confident daily life. The weekly strategies for efficacy follow.

Week One: Start by smiling more to commit to improving your self-efficacy.

Week Two: Engage in a strengths-based challenge.

Week Three: Create a vision board by thinking about what you want to accomplish in your life.

Week Four: Start a personal résumé of your accomplishments and significant moments in your life.

Week Five: Challenge yourself to learn something new.

You can use the reflection and recording tools starting on page 104 as you move through each week's invitation. Before November begins, take time to pause for a brief self-efficacy reflection.

Efficacy Notes and Reflections

Write about current celebrations or challenges regarding your self-efficacy and describe how your improved decision and balance routines from September and October impact your sense of efficacy.

_____

_____

FALL

Nov.

Week One:
Smile More

Invitation: Commit to smiling more this week. Smiling can have a direct impact on your projection of self-confidence. When you smile more, you feel better, are more relaxed, and convey warmth and openness, which can boost your self-confidence with others.

Monday

Tuesday

Wednesday

Learn to smile at every situation. See it as an opportunity to prove your strength and ability.

—Joe Brown

Thursday

Friday

Saturday

Sunday

End-of-Week Wellness Reflections

My celebrations:

_____
_____
_____
_____
_____
_____
_____
_____

My challenges:

_____
_____
_____
_____
_____
_____
_____
_____

My considerations for next week:

_____
_____
_____
_____
_____
_____
_____
_____
_____

Week Two:
Engage in a Strengths Challenge

Invitation: Engage in a strengths-based challenge this week. Write down a minimum of ten things you are good at by using the "Strengths Challenge" tool (page 251) if needed. Continue to add to the list as the week progresses. In addition, consider asking a few trusted friends what they believe you do well.

FALL

Nov.

Monday

Tuesday

Wednesday

Self-confidence is the memory of success.

—David Storey

Thursday

Friday

Saturday

Sunday

My celebrations:

_____
_____
_____
_____
_____
_____
_____
_____

My challenges:

_____
_____
_____
_____
_____
_____
_____
_____

My considerations for next week:

_____
_____
_____
_____
_____
_____
_____
_____
_____

FALL

Nov.

Week Three:
Create a Vision Board

Invitation: Create a vision board by thinking about what you want to accomplish in your life. It could be anything related to your health, finances, relationships, career, education, or travel. Then, set specific goals for yourself to help you begin working toward achieving them. You can use the "My Vision Board" tool (page 252) if needed.

FALL

Nov.

Monday

Tuesday

Wednesday

Nothing builds self-esteem and self-confidence like accomplishment.

— Thomas Carlyle

Thursday

Friday

Saturday

Sunday

End-of-Week Wellness Reflections

My celebrations:

_____

_____

_____

_____

_____

_____

_____

_____

My challenges:

_____

_____

_____

_____

_____

_____

_____

My considerations for next week:

_____

_____

_____

_____

_____

_____

_____

_____

FALL

Nov.

Week Four:
Start a Personal Résumé

Invitation: Start a personal résumé of your accomplishments and significant moments in your life. Think about some of your more significant moments of accomplishment and write them down using the "Personal TA-DA of Accomplishments" tool (page 253) if needed. Keep adding to the list every time you achieve another accomplishment, big or small.

FALL

NOV.

Monday

Tuesday

Wednesday

People with goals succeed because they know where they're going.

—Earl Nightingale

Thursday

Friday

Saturday

Sunday

End-of-Week Wellness Reflections

My celebrations:

_____
_____
_____
_____
_____
_____
_____
_____

My challenges:

_____
_____
_____
_____
_____
_____
_____

My considerations for next week:

_____
_____
_____
_____
_____
_____
_____
_____
_____

FALL

Nov.

Week Five:
Learn Something New

Invitation: Challenge yourself to learn something new. It could be learning new skill; using a new technology; starting a new hobby, language, or sport; or reaching out to make a new friend.

FALL

Nov.

_____
_____
_____
_____
_____
_____
_____
_____
_____

Monday

_____
_____
_____
_____
_____
_____
_____

Tuesday

_____
_____
_____
_____
_____
_____

Wednesday

Inaction breeds doubt and fear. Action breeds confidence and courage. If you want to conquer fear, do not sit at home and think about it. Go out and get busy.

—Dale Carnegie

Thursday

Friday

Saturday

Sunday

End-of-Week Wellness Reflections

My celebrations:

_____
_____
_____

_____
_____
_____
_____
_____

My challenges:

_____
_____
_____

_____
_____
_____
_____

My considerations
for next week:

_____
_____
_____
_____
_____
_____
_____
_____

FALL

Nov.

End-of-Month Reflection: Efficacy Routines

As November ends, pause for a wellness reflection and respond to the following prompts.

1. Reread the five weekly efficacy quotes from this month. Which quote resonated most for you? Why?

_____

_____

_____

_____

2. What did you learn about your efficacy routines this month? What were your celebrations? What were your challenges?

_____

_____

_____

_____

3. Write two *I will* actions regarding your efficacy routines to carry over into December.

   a. I will:

_____

_____

_____

   b. I will:

_____

_____

_____

4. Record any additional thoughts and reflections about your efficacy routines progress this month and how it has impacted your overall sense of confidence in your professional life.

_____

_____

_____

For additional reflection on your efficacy routine progress, go to appendix B (page 277) to self-score your current effort and actions.

_____

_____

_____

_____

_____

_____

_____

_____

_____

_____

_____

_____

_____

_____

_____

_____

_____

_____

_____

_____

_____

_____

_____

_____

_____

_____

FALL

Nov.

End of Fall: What's Next?

As with your physical wellness routines from summer, remember to be patient about your mental wellness routine during the fall months. Small tweaks and minor changes in your decision-making and internal balance routines can add up quickly as you take time out from the daily noise of your work life. Commit to time for a balance reset each day. The Thanksgiving break will be a good time to reflect on your decision-making and self-efficacy progress and perhaps set new goals for developing your confidence and competence for the winter and spring seasons ahead.

You will experience setbacks, and that's OK. The best routines become sustainable when you start with small victories, create greater awareness and understanding of your physical and mental wellness routines, and then set short-term and long-term goals for improvement. View any setbacks as data and use that data as an invitation to keep moving forward, one step at a time.

As you move into winter in the next three months, focus on the emotional wellness dimension of daily life. Your emotions are tied to your actions and reactions, both inside and outside the classroom, and have a primary impact on student learning (Tomlinson & Sousa, 2020). Therefore, your positive response to your emotional state each day opens a portal to cognition and learning for your students, yourself, and your colleagues.

December, January, and February present a *season of perseverance* and the challenge of physical, mental, and emotional weariness as you shift from one semester to the next. The school year's end seems far off. Therefore, during the winter you will explore the daily wellness routines of *awareness, understanding,* and *mindfulness* and how these three emotional wellness routines connect to your work from the summer and fall and help you to remain in a positive emotional state on the most difficult of days.

Ready? Let's go!

Notes

_____

_____

_____

_____

_____

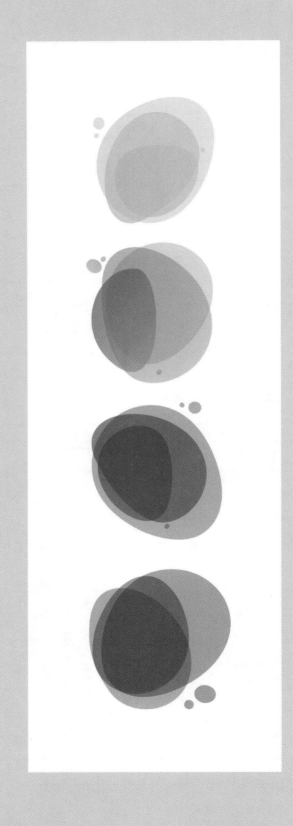

PART 4

WINTER: A SEASON OF PERSEVERANCE

All learning has an emotional base.

—Plato

Winter Overview and Reflection: Emotional Wellness

You begin the winter with the dimension of *emotional* wellness. Your emotions are associated with well-managed stress, greater job satisfaction, and greater student cognition and engagement (Brackett & Simmons, 2015). Your emotions impact your overall mood and how your day feels. Emotional wellness matters just as much as your physical and mental wellness. Winter is a great time to focus on how well you thrive emotionally as you enter a season of perseverance and endurance. Can you sustain a high level of positive emotional energy and inspiration for your students and colleagues during the grind of winter?

According to the Institute for Health and Human Potential (n.d.), emotional intelligence is the ability to "recognize, understand and manage our own emotions," and also "recognize, understand and influence the emotions of others."

Research out of the Yale School of Medicine (n.d.) shows that when a teacher possesses emotional wellness, students cause fewer disruptions, are more focused, and perform better academically. Whether we're interacting with students, colleagues, or families, it's important to consider our emotions and the nature of our responses to them.

For the next three months, you will gain a deeper understanding of the interconnections between the three emotional wellness routines of awareness, understanding, and mindfulness, and the role they play in your daily positive emotional presence in front of your students and colleagues. Each month focuses on the following routines.

- December's emotional wellness routine is *awareness.* Consider how well you identify, track, and respond to your daily emotions.

- January's emotional wellness routine is *understanding.* Consider the *why* behind your emotions and reflect on how you respond to different emotions.

- February's emotional wellness routine is *mindfulness.* Consider how well you use mindfulness practices to respond (positively and thoughtfully) rather than react (negatively and quickly) to your stronger and more unpleasant emotions.

As you begin the season, reflect on and respond to the following prompts.

1. How does focusing on the emotional wellness routines of awareness, understanding, and mindfulness make you feel? For example, do you feel challenged, exhausted, excited, uncertain, or anxious, and why do you feel that way?

_____

_____

_____

_____

2. Reflect on your current personal and professional life. Do you feel that you thrive at work? What helps you to feel good emotionally? What types of emotional self-reflection habits work well for you?

_____

_____

_____

_____

3. What are your current celebrations and challenges around your daily emotional wellness routines of awareness, understanding, and mindfulness?

_____

_____

_____

_____

4. How important are the emotional wellness routines of awareness, understanding, and mindfulness to your closest family members, friends, and colleagues? How might you encourage others to support you or join you as you begin working on your emotional wellness routines over the next three months?

_____

_____

_____

_____

5. Record any additional thoughts and reflections about your current emotional wellness routines and actions.

_____

_____

_____

_____

WINTER

December

Monday	Tuesday	Wednesday

Focus: Awareness Routines (Emotional Wellness)

Thursday	Friday	Saturday	Sunday

WINTER

Dec.

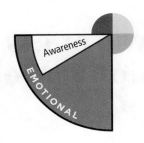

December: Awareness Routines

The focus for December is on your *awareness* routines sometimes referenced as your *emotional awareness* routines. Researchers in psychology and neuroscience indicate that feeling is as important as thinking. Emotions are *mental states* that guide your thoughts, calculations, and decisions (Mlodinow, 2022). Emotions are also *feelings* you experience every day. That means you first become aware of those feelings, reflect on why you are experiencing them, and then appropriately respond. Often you will ignore your emotions and just power through to get through the laundry list of each day's tasks. You push out of mind emotions like anger, fear, sadness, excitement, joy, and tenderness merely because you have too much to do on any given day.

Ignoring your emotions doesn't mean they don't exist. On the contrary, when you pay close attention to your daily emotions, you start to recognize how your moods, interactions, and productivity levels positively impact others.

Each week in December, you are invited to experiment with one strategy for improving your emotional awareness routines. The weekly strategies for awareness follow.

Week One: Track your daily emotions.

Week Two: Monitor your emotional responses to unpleasant emotions.

Week Three: Share strong pleasant emotions such as happiness, joy, and tenderness with others.

Week Four: Write observations about your emotional impact on students or colleagues.

Week Five: Ask students, colleagues, friends, or family members how your daily emotional responses impact others and record their responses.

You can use the reflection and recording tools starting on page 126 as you move through each week's invitation. Before December begins, take time to pause for a brief awareness reflection.

Awareness Notes and Reflections

Write about current celebrations or challenges regarding your emotional awareness routines and describe how those routines impact your daily food and sleep decisions.

_____

_____

Week One:
Track Daily Emotions

Invitation: Track your daily emotions this week, such as anger, sadness, fear, joy, tenderness, or excitement. Pause throughout the day and ask yourself, "What emotions am I experiencing right now?" Write them down. You can use the "Emotions Tracker" tool (page 254) if needed.

_____
_____
_____
_____
_____
_____
_____

Monday

_____
_____
_____
_____
_____
_____
_____

Tuesday

_____
_____
_____
_____
_____

Wednesday

_____
_____
_____
_____
_____

Dec.

WINTER

Knowing yourself is the beginning of all wisdom.

—Aristotle

Thursday

Friday

Saturday

Sunday

End-of-Week Wellness Reflections

My celebrations:

_____
_____
_____
_____
_____
_____
_____
_____
_____
_____

My challenges:

_____
_____
_____
_____
_____
_____
_____
_____
_____

My considerations for next week:

_____
_____
_____
_____
_____
_____
_____
_____

WINTER Dec.

Week Two:
Monitor Emotional Responses

Invitation: Monitor your emotional responses to unpleasant emotions you experience or that others direct toward you this week. Unpleasant emotions include sadness, fear, anxiety, irritation, or anger. You can use the "Unpleasant Emotions Response Tracker" tool (page 255) if needed.

Monday

Tuesday

Wednesday

Dec.

WINTER

If you don't have self-awareness, if you are not able to manage your distressing emotions . . . then no matter how smart you are, you are not going to get very far.

—Daniel Goleman

Thursday

Friday

Saturday

Sunday

End-of-Week Wellness Reflections

My celebrations:

_____
_____
_____
_____
_____
_____
_____
_____
_____

My challenges:

_____
_____
_____
_____
_____
_____
_____

My considerations for next week:

_____
_____
_____
_____
_____
_____
_____
_____

WINTER

Dec.

Week Three:
Share Pleasant Emotions

Invitation: Notice how often you share strong, pleasant emotions such as happiness, joy, and tenderness with others this week. Be intentional about validating and celebrating other people expressing their pleasant emotions and feelings. You can use the "Pleasant Emotions Tracker" tool (page 256) if needed.

_____

Monday

Tuesday

Wednesday

> Connection is the energy that exists between people when they feel seen, heard, and valued.
>
> —Brené Brown

Thursday

Friday

Saturday

Sunday

End-of-Week Wellness Reflections

My celebrations:

_____
_____
_____
_____
_____
_____
_____
_____
_____

My challenges:

_____
_____
_____
_____
_____
_____
_____
_____

My considerations
for next week:

_____
_____
_____
_____
_____
_____
_____
_____
_____

WINTER Dec.

Week Four:
Observe Emotional Impact

Invitation: Describe a moment from each day when you noticed your positive emotional impact on the learning, perseverance, or effort of others. Moments can include a story you told, words of affirmation you said, joy and grace toward others that you modeled, or a thank-you note you wrote. You can use the "Impact of Your Emotions on Others" tool (page 257) if needed.

Monday

Tuesday

Wednesday

Dec.

WINTER

If we can learn to identify, express, and harness our feelings . . . we can use emotions to help us create positive, satisfying lives.

—Marc Brackett

Thursday

Friday

Saturday

Sunday

End-of-Week Wellness Reflections

My celebrations:

_____
_____
_____
_____
_____
_____
_____
_____

My challenges:

_____
_____
_____
_____
_____
_____
_____

My considerations for next week:

_____
_____
_____
_____
_____
_____

WINTER

Dec.

Week Five:
Get Emotional Response Feedback

Invitation: Ask students, colleagues, friends, or family members: "Is my daily emotional response generally positive toward others? Why or why not?" You can use the "Emotional Response Feedback" tool (page 258) if needed.

Monday

_____

Tuesday

WINTER

Dec.

Wednesday

The greatest compliment that was ever paid to me was when one asked me what I thought, and attended to my answer.

— Henry David Thoreau

Thursday

Friday

Saturday

Sunday

End-of-Week Wellness Reflections

My celebrations:

_____
_____
_____
_____
_____
_____
_____
_____

My challenges:

_____
_____
_____
_____
_____
_____
_____

My considerations for next week:

_____
_____
_____
_____
_____
_____
_____

WINTER Dec.

End-of-Month Reflection: Awareness Routines

As December ends, pause for an emotional awareness reflection and respond to the following prompts.

1. Reread the five weekly emotional awareness quotes from this month. Which quote resonated most for you? Why?

_____

_____

_____

_____

2. What did you learn about your own emotional awareness routines this month? What were your celebrations? What were your challenges?

_____

_____

_____

_____

3. Write two *I will* actions regarding your emotional awareness routines to carry over into January:

   a. I will:

   _____

   _____

   _____

   _____

   b. I will:

   _____

   _____

   _____

   _____

4. Record any additional thoughts and reflections about your progress this month and how it impacted your physical and mental wellness routines.

_____

_____

_____

_____

Dec.

WINTER

For additional reflection on your emotional awareness routine progress, go to appendix B (page 277) to self-score your current effort and actions.

Notes

_____

_____

_____

_____

_____

_____

_____

_____

_____

_____

_____

_____

_____

_____

_____

_____

_____

_____

_____

_____

_____

_____

_____

_____

_____

_____

_____

_____

_____

_____

_____

_____

WINTER Dec.

January

Monday	Tuesday	Wednesday

Focus: Understanding Routines (Emotional Wellness)

Thursday	Friday	Saturday	Sunday

WINTER

Jan.

January: Understanding Routines

The focus for January is on your *understanding* routines sometimes referenced as your *emotional understanding* routines. Understanding your emotions begins when you uncover the *why* behind the emotions. When you recognize your emotions and are aware of your responses to them (your December wellness work), you begin to understand what or who evokes pleasant and unpleasant emotions. This understanding is important not because you can avoid these events or people altogether but because you can become more aware of your emotional triggers. Why do you feel the way you do throughout your day? What situations cause you to experience certain emotions, and what do you do when you experience those emotions? By understanding your emotions better, you strengthen your emotional wellness and intelligence.

Each week in January, you are invited to experiment with one strategy for improving your emotional understanding routines and avoiding a negative energy life. The weekly strategies for emotional understanding follow.

Week One: Identify triggers to your happy and excited emotions.

Week Two: Identify triggers to your more unpleasant emotions.

Week Three: Identify patterns connected to your daily emotions.

Week Four: Participate in a daily challenge to support a positive response when unpleasant emotions surface.

Week Five: Practice modeling healthy emotional responses.

You can use the reflection and recording tools starting on page 142 as you move through each week's invitation. Before January begins, take time to pause for a brief emotional understanding reflection.

Understanding Notes and Reflections

Write about current celebrations or challenges regarding your emotional understanding routines and describe how those routines impact your positive emotional energy throughout the day.

_____

_____

Week One:
Identify Pleasant Emotion Triggers

Invitation: Identify work-life experiences that trigger your happier and more excited emotions. Similar to your emotional awareness actions in December, track each moment you experienced a pleasant emotion and describe what happened just before feeling that emotion. You can use the "Pleasant Emotion Triggers" tool (page 259) if needed.

Monday

Tuesday

Wednesday

WINTER

Jan.

He who smiles rather than rages is always the stronger.

—**Japanese proverb**

Thursday

Friday

Saturday

Sunday

End-of-Week Wellness Reflections

My celebrations:

_____
_____
_____
_____
_____
_____
_____
_____
_____

My challenges:

_____
_____
_____
_____
_____
_____
_____

My considerations for next week:

_____
_____
_____
_____
_____
_____

WINTER

Jan.

Week Two:
Identify Unpleasant Emotion Triggers

Invitation: Identify events that trigger unpleasant emotions. Unpleasant emotions include sadness, anger, anxiety, fear, rejection, and others. Track each time you experience an unpleasant emotion and describe what happened just before the emotion surfaced. You can use the "Unpleasant Emotion Triggers" tool (page 260) if needed.

Monday

Tuesday

Wednesday

WINTER

Jan.

So the first step in seeking happiness is learning. We first have to learn how negative emotions and behaviors are harmful to us and how positive emotions are helpful.

—**Fourteenth Dalai Lama**

Thursday

Friday

Saturday

Sunday

End-of-Week Wellness Reflections

My celebrations:

_____
_____
_____
_____
_____
_____
_____
_____

My challenges:

_____
_____
_____
_____
_____
_____

My considerations for next week:

_____
_____
_____
_____
_____
_____

WINTER

Jan.

Week Three:
Identify Emotion Patterns

Invitation: When an event or situation occurs during your day that causes an unpleasant emotional response, pause for ninety seconds. Commit to using the ninety-second pause to reflect on the *what* and *why* of the emotion you are experiencing at that moment.

Monday

Tuesday

WINTER

Jan.

Wednesday

I don't want to be at the mercy of my emotions. I want to use them, to enjoy them, and to dominate them.

—Oscar Wilde

Thursday

Friday

Saturday

Sunday

End-of-Week Wellness Reflections

My celebrations:

_____
_____
_____
_____
_____
_____
_____
_____

My challenges:

_____
_____
_____
_____
_____
_____
_____
_____

My considerations for next week:

_____
_____
_____
_____
_____
_____
_____
_____

Week Four:
Commit to Healthy Emotional Responses

Invitation: Monitor situations that cause you to experience unpleasant emotions, such as driving, reading social media comments, or hearing certain words or phrases said by a student, family member, or friend. Make it a challenge to not overreact in the moment. You can use the "My Daily Challenge Commitment" tool (page 261) if needed.

Monday

Tuesday

Wednesday

WINTER

Jan.

> The sign of an intelligent people is their ability to control emotions by the application of reason.
>
> —Marya Mannes

Thursday

Friday

Saturday

Sunday

End-of-Week Wellness Reflections

My celebrations:
_____
_____
_____
_____
_____
_____
_____
_____
_____

My challenges:
_____
_____
_____
_____
_____
_____

My considerations for next week:
_____
_____
_____
_____
_____
_____
_____
_____

WINTER
Jan.

Week Five:
Model Healthy Emotional Responses

Invitation: Accept the "ten things you are grateful for" challenge. Write about people, places, moments, or activities in your daily life that make you happy. Reflect each day on how you can model healthy emotional responses to others. You can use the "I'm Grateful For" tool (page 262) if needed.

_____

_____

_____

_____

_____

_____

_____

_____

_____

Monday

_____

_____

_____

_____

_____

_____

_____

_____

_____

Tuesday

_____

_____

_____

_____

Wednesday

_____

_____

_____

_____

_____

WINTER

Jan.

Gratitude is the healthiest of all human emotions. The more you express gratitude for what you have, the more likely you will have even more to express gratitude for.

—Zig Ziglar

Thursday

Friday

Saturday

Sunday

End-of-Week Wellness Reflections

My celebrations:

_____
_____
_____
_____
_____
_____
_____
_____
_____

My challenges:

_____
_____
_____
_____
_____
_____
_____
_____

My considerations for next week:

_____
_____
_____
_____
_____
_____
_____

WINTER
Jan.

End-of-Month Reflection: Understanding Routines

As January ends, pause for a wellness reflection and respond to the following prompts.

1. Reread the five weekly understanding quotes from this month. Which quote resonated most for you? Why?

_____

_____

_____

_____

2. What did you learn about your emotional understanding routines this month? What were your celebrations? What were your challenges?

_____

_____

_____

_____

3. Write two *I will* actions regarding your emotional understanding routines to carry over into February.

   a. I will:

_____

_____

_____

_____

   b. I will:

_____

_____

_____

_____

4. Record any additional thoughts and reflections about your progress this month and how it impacted your decision-making, balance, and self-efficacy mental wellness routines from fall.

_____

_____

_____

_____

WINTER

Jan.

For additional reflection on your emotional understanding routine progress, go to appendix B (page 277) to self-score your current effort and actions.

Notes

_____

_____

_____

_____

_____

_____

_____

_____

_____

_____

_____

_____

_____

_____

_____

_____

_____

_____

_____

_____

_____

_____

_____

_____

_____

_____

_____

_____

_____

_____

_____

WINTER

Jan.

February

Monday	Tuesday	Wednesday

WINTER

Feb.

Focus: Mindfulness Routines (Emotional Wellness)

Thursday	Friday	Saturday	Sunday

WINTER

Feb.

February: Mindfulness Routines

The focus for February is on your *mindfulness* routines now that you've built awareness routines around your emotions. Mindfulness routines help you respond effectively and not merely react to your emotions. Mindfulness routines can become an essential tool for calming your more unpleasant emotions to reach a state of mind where you can positively respond rather than negatively react toward others. Your mindfulness routines are an emotional management tool. Just as you work to improve your physical and mental well-being, your mindfulness routines help you to improve your emotional well-being.

Each week in February, you are invited to experiment with one strategy for improving your mindfulness routines and help you avoid negative reactions to the emotions you experience each day. The weekly strategies for mindfulness follow.

Week One: Notice when you react versus when you respond to your emotions.

Week Two: Practice mindful breathing.

Week Three: Practice meditation.

Week Four: Experiment with journaling.

Week Five: Take a mindful walk.

You can use the reflection and recording tools starting on page 158 as you move through each week's invitation. Before February begins, take time to pause for a brief mindfulness reflection.

Mindfulness Notes and Reflections

Write about current celebrations or challenges regarding your mindfulness routines and describe how those routines impact your daily decision-making, balance, and efficacy routines from the fall mental wellness focus.

_____

_____

_____

_____

_____

_____

Week One:
Notice React Versus Respond

Invitation: Notice when you react versus when you respond to your emotions and the emotions of others this week. Pay attention to how you feel when you react (negatively and quickly) versus when you respond (positively and thoughtfully) and the factors that lead to each reaction or response. You can use the "React Versus Respond Reflections" tool (page 263) if needed.

Monday

Tuesday

WINTER

Feb.

Wednesday

Wherever you are, be there totally.

—Eckhart Tolle

Thursday

Friday

Saturday

Sunday

End-of-Week Wellness Reflections

My celebrations:

_____

_____

_____

_____

_____

_____

_____

_____

My challenges:

_____

_____

_____

_____

_____

_____

_____

My considerations for next week:

_____

_____

_____

_____

_____

_____

_____

WINTER

Feb.

Week Two:
Practice Mindful Breathing

Invitation: Try daily mindful breathing this week. Simply focus your attention on your breath as you inhale and exhale. For example, try to push your breath into your belly so that your stomach expands on the inhale. Pay attention to (and possibly record) how you feel before and after you pause for a mindful breath.

Monday

Tuesday

Wednesday

WINTER

Feb.

Mindfulness isn't difficult. We just need to remember to do it.

—Sharon Salzberg

Thursday

Friday

Saturday

Sunday

End-of-Week Wellness Reflections

My celebrations:

_____
_____
_____
_____
_____
_____
_____
_____

My challenges:

_____
_____
_____
_____
_____
_____
_____
_____

My considerations for next week:

_____
_____
_____
_____
_____
_____
_____
_____
_____

WINTER

Feb.

Week Three:
Practice Meditation

Invitation: Try meditation this week. Like last week, meditation is about focusing on your breath and staying in the present moment, but it requires a bit more time. Try a guided meditation through the UCLA Mindful Awareness Research Center (www.uclahealth.org/programs/marc) or download a meditation app with a free trial such as Headspace (www.headspace.com) or Calm (www.calm.com).

Monday

Tuesday

WINTER

Feb.

Wednesday

Life is a dance. Mindfulness is witnessing that dance.

—Amit Ray

Thursday

Friday

Saturday

Sunday

End-of-Week Wellness Reflections

My celebrations:

_____
_____
_____
_____
_____
_____
_____
_____
_____

My challenges:

_____
_____
_____
_____
_____
_____
_____

My considerations for next week:

_____
_____
_____
_____
_____
_____

WINTER

Feb.

Week Four:
Experiment With Journaling

Invitation: Try experimenting with journaling this week. Try a brain dump, where you write whatever you're thinking without worrying about editing yourself or your writing. You can also doodle or color. Just do something that helps you move your thoughts and feelings out of your head and down on paper. You can use the "Journal Experimenting" tool (page 264) if needed.

Monday

Tuesday

Wednesday

WINTER

Feb.

How we pay attention to the present moment largely determines the character of our experience, and therefore, the quality of our lives.

—Sam Harris

Thursday

Friday

Saturday

Sunday

My celebrations:

_____
_____
_____
_____
_____
_____
_____
_____
_____

My challenges:

_____
_____
_____
_____
_____
_____
_____

My considerations for next week:

_____
_____
_____
_____
_____
_____
_____

WINTER

Feb.

Week Five:
Take a Mindful Walk

Invitation: Take a mindful walk this week. For some people, movement is a tool for emotional wellness. Choose a path where you can take an uninterrupted ten-minute walk without distraction. Pay attention to your emotions before, during, and after your walk. You can use the "Mindful Walking Emotions" tool (page 265) if needed.

_____

Monday

_____

Tuesday

WINTER

Feb.

Wednesday

Training your mind to be in the present moment is the number one key to making healthier choices.

—Susan Albers

Thursday

Friday

Saturday

Sunday

My celebrations:

_____
_____
_____
_____
_____
_____
_____
_____
_____
_____

My challenges:

_____
_____
_____
_____
_____
_____
_____
_____
_____

My considerations for next week:

_____
_____
_____
_____
_____
_____
_____
_____

WINTER

Feb.

End-of-Month Reflection: Mindfulness Routines

As February ends, pause for a mindfulness reflection and respond to the following prompts.

1. Reread the five weekly mindfulness quotes from this month. Which quote resonated most for you? Why?

_____

_____

_____

_____

2. What did you learn about your mindfulness routines this month? What were your celebrations? What were your challenges?

_____

_____

_____

_____

3. Write two *I will* actions regarding your mindfulness routines to carry over into March.

    a. I will:

_____

_____

_____

_____

    b. I will:

_____

_____

_____

_____

4. Record any additional thoughts and reflections about your mindfulness routine progress this month and how it may have impacted your decision-making routines.

_____

_____

_____

WINTER

Feb.

For additional reflection on your mindfulness routine progress, go to appendix B (page 277) to self-score your current effort and actions.

Notes

_____
_____
_____
_____
_____
_____
_____
_____
_____
_____
_____
_____
_____
_____
_____
_____
_____
_____
_____
_____
_____
_____
_____
_____
_____
_____
_____
_____
_____
_____

WINTER

Feb.

End of Winter: What's Next?

As with your physical and mental wellness routines from the summer and fall, remember it is important to be patient with yourself and understand how small tweaks and minor changes in your mindfulness routines can add up quickly. As you consider the emotional wellness routines that served you well this winter, be sure to continue to take time to respond positively, and not react negatively, to your daily experienced emotions.

Use the spring months to get outside more and take a walk or mental break to reflect on how you hope to finish the school year with a sustained positive emotional impact on your students and colleagues. Of course, there will be occasional emotional setbacks. There always are, and that's OK. Remember, the best routines become sustainable when you start with small victories, improve awareness and understanding of your emotions, and set short- and long-term goals for improvement. View any setbacks as data and use those data as a challenge to keep moving forward—one step at a time.

During the next season, your focus will be on the *social wellness* dimension of daily life. We need positive social connections to thrive in our first three dimensions of wellness. Our social wellness serves our physical, mental, and emotional wellness, and vice versa. Students, colleagues, friends, and family are more likely to desire social connection with us when we are in a positive emotional space.

The spring months of March, April, and May present a *season of transition* and the challenges of sustaining positive relationships, building and maintaining trust, and staying connected to your purpose as you prepare for the end of the school year. Your mantra becomes *finish this school year well.* You move into social wellness routines that allow you to stay strong for yourself, your colleagues, and most of all your students. You will explore the daily wellness routines of *relationship, trust,* and *purpose* and how these routines can help you become the kind of educator others want to be around every day.

Ready? Let's go!

Notes

_____

_____

_____

_____

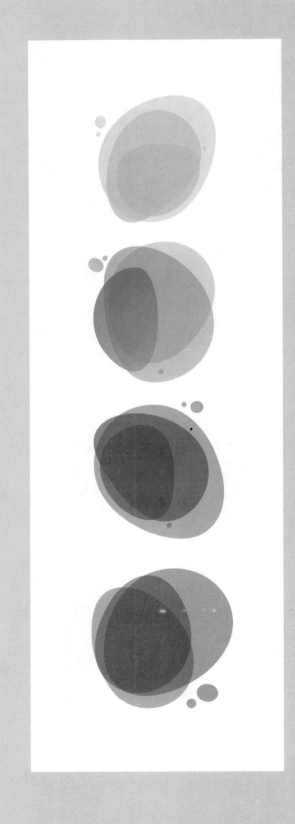

PART 5

SPRING: A SEASON OF TRANSITION

Close relationships, more than money or fame, are what keep
people happy throughout their lives. . . . Those ties protect
people from life's discontents, help to delay mental and
physical decline, and are better predictors of long and happy
lives than social class, IQ, or even genes.

—Harvard Medical School

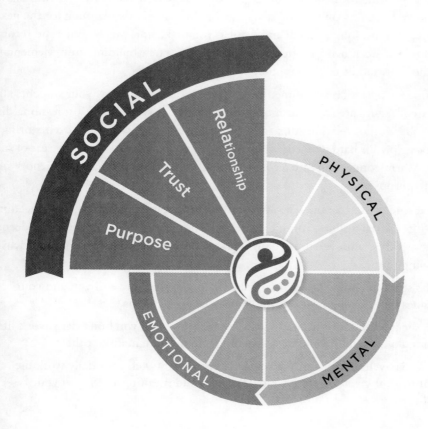

Spring Overview and Reflection: Social Wellness

You begin spring, the season of wellness, with the fourth dimension of the Wellness Solutions for Educators framework: *social wellness*. Daniel Goleman (2006) describes how "our social interactions play a role in reshaping our brain, through neuroplasticity, which means that repeated experiences [with others] sculpt the shape, size, and number of neurons and their synaptic connections" (p. 11). Goleman (2006) defines your social intelligence as a "shorthand term for being intelligent not just about our relationships, but also in them" (p. 323).

Spring is a great time to focus on how to thrive socially at work as you set your sights on the challenges of ending one school season while simultaneously planning for the next. There is a sense of transition in March and April as you make final preparations and recommendations for students moving to the next grade level, to a new building, from elementary to middle school or middle to high school, or on to graduation.

May is a time for reflection and sometimes anxiety because you know your students and some of your colleagues are about to move on. Each school year of your professional life is a distinct collection of relationships and deep connections. Graduation events bring a sense of purpose to your hard work and remind you of the beneficiaries of your year of sustained effort. Warm connections are a core feature of our optimal human experiences and serve our core purpose.

For the next three months, you will gain a deeper understanding of the interconnections between the three social wellness routines of relationship, trust, and purpose. These deeper wellness actions will sustain you amid daily work and life challenges. Each month focuses on the following routines.

- March's social wellness routine is *relationship*. Consider how well you and your colleagues build strong relationships and social connections together.

- April's social wellness routine is *trust*. Consider how well you build daily work-life routines of vulnerability and deep listening without judgment of others.

- May's social wellness routine is *purpose*. Consider how well your daily work life feeds into your greater purpose and helps you find meaning and joy in your work life.

As you begin the season, reflect on and respond to the following prompts.

1. How does focusing on the social wellness routines of relationship, trust, and purpose make you feel? For example, do you feel challenged, ready to go, excited, or uncertain, and why do you feel that way?

_____

_____

_____

_____

2. Reflect on your current personal and professional life. What current relationships have helped you thrive at work? How did you develop trust in those relationships? How did those relationships help you stay connected to your purpose as an educator?

_____

_____

_____

_____

3. What are your current celebrations and challenges around your daily social wellness routines of relationship, trust, and purpose actions?

_____

_____

_____

_____

4. How important are the social wellness routines of relationship, trust, and purpose to your closest family members, friends, and colleagues? How might you encourage others to support or join you as you begin working over the next three months on your social wellness routines?

_____

_____

_____

_____

5. Record any additional thoughts and reflections about your current social wellness routines and actions.

_____

_____

_____

_____

SPRING

March

Monday	Tuesday	Wednesday

Focus: Relationship Routines (Social Wellness)

Thursday	Friday	Saturday	Sunday

SPRING

March

March: Relationship Routines

The focus for March is on your *relationship* routines. By investing time in others, maximizing your strengths to benefit one another, and encouraging your colleagues to persevere through the hard work of student success, you begin to experience intimacy in your work life. Mutually nourishing relationships become the norm.

We feel our best when our relationships are positive, as there is an increased sense of satisfaction, safety, and comfort at work. Yale University lecturer Emma Seppälä and Yale University professor Marissa King (2017) indicate that an outcome of becoming more socially connected is an increase in our mental well-being and self-esteem. Thus, our road to social wellness runs through our willingness to create a culture of belonging and inclusion with our students and colleagues.

Each week in March, you are invited to experiment with one strategy for improving your relationship-building skills. The weekly strategies for relationship building follow.

Week One: Write a thank-you note to three students or colleagues.

Week Two: Ask a colleague to go for a thirty-minute walk and talk.

Week Three: Write a one-page gratitude note to a colleague.

Week Four: Ask a trusted colleague, "What is it like to be you today?"

Week Five: Make a list of colleagues, friends, and family members in your inner circle.

You can use the reflection and recording tools starting on page 180 as you move through each week's invitation. Before March begins, take time to pause for a brief relationship-building reflection.

Relationship Notes and Reflections

Write about current celebrations or challenges regarding your relationship-building routines and describe how your current relationships impact your sense of confidence and competence (self-efficacy) at work.

_____

_____

_____

_____

SPRING

March

Week One:
Write Thank-You Notes

Invitation: Write a thank-you note (digital or handwritten) to three students or colleagues this week. Give them the notes without any expectation for a return response. You can use the "Thank-You Notes" tool (page 266) if needed.

Monday

Tuesday

Wednesday

Don't let the sun go down
without saying thank you to
someone, and without admitting
to yourself absolutely no one
gets this far alone.

—Stephen King

Thursday

Friday

Saturday

Sunday

End-of-Week Wellness Reflections

My celebrations:

_____
_____
_____
_____
_____
_____
_____

My challenges:

_____
_____
_____
_____
_____
_____

My considerations for next week:

_____
_____
_____
_____
_____
_____
_____

SPRING

March

Week Two:
Go for a Walk and Talk

Invitation: Ask one or several colleagues to go for a thirty-minute walk and talk (outside if possible) and spend time sharing celebrations and challenges at work or at home (if appropriate).

Monday

Tuesday

Wednesday

> I am not the smartest fellow in the world, but I sure can pick smart colleagues.
>
> —Franklin Roosevelt

Thursday

Friday

Saturday

Sunday

End-of-Week Wellness Reflections

My celebrations:

_____
_____
_____
_____
_____
_____
_____
_____

My challenges:

_____
_____
_____
_____
_____
_____
_____

My considerations for next week:

_____
_____
_____
_____
_____
_____
_____
_____

SPRING   March

Week Three:
Write a Gratitude Note

Invitation: Write a one-page gratitude note to a colleague this week. Ask them for thirty minutes before or after school or ask them out for coffee or tea. When ready, read your note to them without interruption. Let the conversation follow. When finished, give them a copy of what you wrote. You can use the "Gratitude Note" tool (page 267) if needed.

Monday

Tuesday

Wednesday

In the sweetness of friendship let there be laughter, and the sharing of pleasures. For in the dew of little things the heart finds its morning and is refreshed.

—**Kahlil Gibran**

Thursday

Friday

Saturday

Sunday

End-of-Week Wellness Reflections

My celebrations:

_____
_____
_____
_____
_____
_____
_____
_____

My challenges:

_____
_____
_____
_____
_____
_____
_____

My considerations for next week:

_____
_____
_____
_____
_____
_____
_____

SPRING March

Week Four:
Build Relationship With a Colleague

Invitation: Ask a trusted colleague to respond to "What is it like to be you today?" Listen without judgment or interruption. Tell them what you heard when they finish and explain why you enjoy working with them each day.

Monday

Tuesday

Wednesday

When I is replaced by we, even illness becomes wellness.

—Charles Roppel

Thursday

Friday

Saturday

Sunday

My celebrations:

_____
_____
_____
_____
_____
_____
_____
_____

My challenges:

_____
_____
_____
_____
_____
_____
_____

My considerations for next week:

_____
_____
_____
_____
_____
_____
_____

SPRING March

Week Five:
Identify Inner Circle

Invitation: Write a list of all colleagues, friends, and family members in your closest inner circle who challenge and inspire you. Then, list three intentional actions you can take during April to spend more time with them. You can use the "My Inner Circle" tool (page 268) if needed.

_____
_____
_____
_____
_____
_____
_____
_____

Monday

_____
_____
_____
_____
_____
_____
_____
_____

Tuesday

_____
_____
_____
_____
_____
_____

Wednesday

_____
_____
_____
_____
_____
_____

Find a group of people who challenge and inspire you, spend a lot of time with them, and it will change your life.

—Amy Poehler

Thursday

Friday

Saturday

Sunday

End-of-Week Wellness Reflections

My celebrations:

_____
_____
_____
_____
_____
_____
_____
_____
_____

My challenges:

_____
_____
_____
_____
_____
_____
_____
_____

My considerations for next week:

_____
_____
_____
_____
_____
_____
_____

SPRING   March

End-of-Month Reflection:
Relationship Routines

As March ends, pause for a wellness reflection and respond to the following prompts.

1. Reread the five weekly relationship quotes from this month. Which quote resonated most for you? Why?

_____

_____

_____

_____

2. What did you learn about your relationship routines this month? What were your celebrations? What were your challenges?

_____

_____

_____

_____

3. Write two *I will* actions regarding your relationship routines to carry over into April.

   a. I will:

   _____

   _____

   _____

   b. I will:

   _____

   _____

   _____

4. Record any additional thoughts and reflections about how your relationship-building progress this month impacted your emotional wellness routines of awareness, understanding, and mindfulness from the winter.

March

SPRING

For additional reflection on your relationship routine progress, go to appendix B (page 277) to self-score your current effort and actions.

Notes

SPRING March

April

Monday	Tuesday	Wednesday

Focus: Trust Routines
(Social Wellness)

Thursday	Friday	Saturday	Sunday

SPRING

April

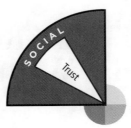

April: Trust Routines

The focus for April is on your *trust* routines. You continue the season of social wellness with this focus because trust is mutually nourishing and trust routines can help you become a trustworthy person for students, colleagues, family, and friends. Trust can make your relationships positive, strong, and respectful. The lack of trust can make your relationships weak, superficial, or dysfunctional.

Perhaps surprisingly, vulnerability is a precursor to trust (Zak, 2017). Vulnerability creates and strengthens a trust culture throughout your team, classroom, school, or district. We develop routines for vulnerability when both the giver (I'll signal my vulnerability to you) and the receiver (you'll hopefully accept, instead of reject, my request for help) interact in a positive communication cycle. By learning how to trust others and to be trustworthy, you can develop positive, strong, and respectful relationships in your work and personal life.

Each week in April, you are invited to experiment with one strategy for improving your trust routines. The weekly strategies for trust follow.

Week One: Avoid gossip to build trust with colleagues.

Week Two: Listen without judgment of others.

Week Three: Show vulnerability by apologizing.

Week Four: Ask others for help, wisdom, or advice.

Week Five: Take initiative to model and build trust with students and colleagues.

You can use the reflection and recording tools starting on page 196 as you move through each week's invitation. Before April begins, take time to pause for a brief trust reflection.

Trust Notes and Reflections

Write about current celebrations or challenges regarding your trust routines and describe how your sense of trust is impacted by your improved relationship-building routines from March.

_____

_____

_____

_____

_____

SPRING

April

Week One:
Avoid Gossip

Invitation: Trust builders avoid gossip and negative talk about others. This week, when others talk negatively or complain about other people, walk away. If needed, consider working with a few colleagues to establish new norms for eliminating gossiping, whining, and complaining about others in your school or district classrooms, hallways, or offices.

Monday

Tuesday

Wednesday

> Great minds discuss ideas.
> Average minds discuss
> events. Small minds
> discuss people.
>
> —Unknown

Thursday

Friday

Saturday

Sunday

End-of-Week Wellness Reflections

My celebrations:

_____
_____
_____
_____
_____
_____
_____
_____
_____

My challenges:

_____
_____
_____
_____
_____
_____
_____
_____

My considerations for next week:

_____
_____
_____
_____
_____
_____
_____
_____

SPRING

April

Week Two:
Listen Without Interruption

Invitation: Trust builders listen more than they talk. This week, listen without interrupting and commit to talking less. Take notice each day of how often you interrupt others. Demonstrate active listening by giving your undivided attention during conversations. You can use the "Listening Without Interrupting" tool (page 269) if needed.

Monday

Tuesday

Wednesday

SPRING

April

Most people do not
listen with the intent to
understand; they listen
with the intent to reply.

—Stephen Covey

Thursday

Friday

Saturday

Sunday

End-of-Week Wellness Reflections

My celebrations:

_____
_____
_____
_____
_____
_____
_____
_____
_____
_____

My challenges:

_____
_____
_____
_____
_____
_____
_____
_____
_____

My considerations for next week:

_____
_____
_____
_____
_____
_____
_____
_____
_____

SPRING

April

Week Three:
Show Vulnerability by Apologizing

Invitation: Trust builders are vulnerable. They apologize when they make a mistake. Practice apologizing to a student, colleague, friend, or family member. You can use the "Apology Reflections" tool (page 270) if needed.

Monday

Tuesday

Wednesday

A real apology requires freely admitting fault, fully accepting responsibility, humbly asking forgiveness, immediately changing behavior, actively rebuilding trust.

—Unknown

Thursday

Friday

Saturday

Sunday

End-of-Week Wellness Reflections

My celebrations:

_____

_____

_____

_____

_____

_____

_____

_____

My challenges:

_____

_____

_____

_____

_____

_____

_____

_____

My considerations for next week:

_____

_____

_____

_____

_____

_____

_____

_____

_____

SPRING

April

Week Four:
Ask for Help

Invitation: Trust builders ask for help and see it as a strength, not a weakness. This week, commit to asking for help. It's OK to admit if you need help with someone or something. Commit each day to ask for someone else's wisdom or advice. Remember, you don't have to know everything. You build trust when you are open to learning from others.

_____

Monday

Tuesday

Wednesday

Accepting help is a sign of strength; asking for it is a sign of maturity.

—Tal Gur

Thursday

Friday

Saturday

Sunday

My celebrations:

_____
_____
_____
_____
_____
_____
_____
_____
_____

My challenges:

_____
_____
_____
_____
_____
_____
_____
_____

My considerations for next week:

_____
_____
_____
_____
_____
_____
_____
_____

SPRING

April

Week Five:
Model and Build Trust

Invitation: Trust builders seek ways to help those around them. This week, take the initiative to help someone without being asked, including for an area of responsibility that might be outside your normal duties. Look for any issues or challenging situations, and then take action to help students or colleagues solve the problem. You can use the "Taking Initiative" tool (page 271) if needed.

_____

Monday

_____

Tuesday

_____

Wednesday

Trust is the ability for everyone in an organization to confidently rely on (and predict) that others will do the right thing and make good on their promises.

— **Marie-Claire Ross**

Thursday

Friday

Saturday

Sunday

End-of-Week Wellness Reflections

My celebrations:
_____
_____
_____
_____
_____
_____
_____
_____

My challenges:
_____
_____
_____
_____
_____
_____
_____
_____

My considerations for next week:
_____
_____
_____
_____
_____
_____

SPRING
April

End-of-Month Reflection: Trust Routines

As April ends, pause for a wellness reflection and respond to the following prompts.

1. Reread the five weekly trust quotes from this month. Which quote resonated most for you? Why?

_____

_____

_____

_____

2. What did you learn about your trust-building routines this month? What were your celebrations? What were your challenges?

_____

_____

_____

_____

3. Write two *I will* actions regarding your trust-building routines to carry over into May.

   a. I will:

_____

_____

_____

   b. I will:

_____

_____

_____

4. Record any additional thoughts and reflections about your progress and how your trust routines this month impact your relationship routines from March.

_____

_____

_____

_____

SPRING

April

For additional reflection on your trust routine progress, go to appendix B (page 277) to self-score your current effort and actions.

Notes

_____

_____

_____

_____

_____

_____

_____

_____

_____

_____

_____

_____

_____

_____

_____

_____

_____

_____

_____

_____

_____

_____

_____

_____

_____

_____

_____

May

Monday	Tuesday	Wednesday

Focus: Purpose Routines (Social Wellness)

Thursday	Friday	Saturday	Sunday

SPRING

May

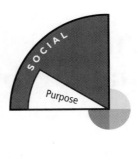

May: Purpose Routines

The focus for May is on your *purpose* routines. Connecting to your purpose for working in this profession helps you thrive in your stewardship of the social and emotional welfare of your students and colleagues. Your profession expects a lot from you and needs you to stay connected to your purpose.

You pursue your educator wellness because it allows you to live your best life each day in a profession that serves your greater purpose. By exploring each of the previous routines, you set yourself up to live your purpose out loud each day. The past two months asked you to focus on relationships and trust, which are rooted in improving the quality of your connections with others. You honor your purpose as an educator by understanding your role in building high-quality, incredible relationships as you work to improve the lives of students and colleagues.

Each week in May, you are invited to experiment with one strategy for connecting to your purpose. The weekly strategies for exploring purpose follow.

Week One: Write about who you are as an educator.

Week Two: Consider your deepest desires as an educator.

Week Three: Identify your purpose as an educator and write about *why* you chose the profession.

Week Four: Remember to connect to your purpose.

Week Five: Share your purpose with others.

You can use the reflection and recording tools starting on page 212 as you move through each week's invitations. Before May begins, take time to pause for a brief purpose reflection.

Purpose Notes and Reflections

Write about current celebrations or challenges regarding your purpose routines and describe how knowing your purpose as an educator can deepen your relationships at work and home.

_____

_____

_____

_____

SPRING

May

Week One:
Discover Who You Are as an Educator

Invitation: Consider who you are as an educator this week. Use your mindfulness routines to pause and reflect. Pay attention to any sensations, images, feelings, or thoughts that come to you. Then, write who you are as an educator in ten words or fewer. You can use the "Who Are You as an Educator?" tool (page 272) if needed.

Monday

Tuesday

Wednesday

SPRING

May

> Our prime purpose in this life is to help others. And if you can't help them, at least don't hurt them.
>
> —Fourteenth Dalai Lama

Thursday

Friday

Saturday

Sunday

My celebrations:
_____
_____
_____
_____
_____
_____
_____
_____

My challenges:
_____
_____
_____
_____
_____
_____
_____

My considerations for next week:
_____
_____
_____
_____
_____
_____
_____
_____

SPRING

May

Week Two:
Consider Your Desires as an Educator

Invitation: Consider your deepest desires as an educator. Again, using your mindfulness routines, pause and reflect. What is it that you want as an educator? Allow any sensations, images, feelings, or thoughts to come to you. You can use the "What Are Your Deepest Desires as an Educator?" tool (page 273) if needed.

_____
_____
_____
_____
_____
_____
_____
_____

Monday

_____
_____
_____
_____
_____
_____
_____

Tuesday

_____
_____
_____
_____
_____
_____

Wednesday

_____
_____
_____
_____
_____
_____

Effort and courage are not enough without purpose and direction.

—John F. Kennedy

Thursday

Friday

Saturday

Sunday

End-of-Week Wellness Reflections

My celebrations:

_____
_____
_____
_____
_____
_____
_____

My challenges:

_____
_____
_____
_____
_____
_____
_____

My considerations for next week:

_____
_____
_____
_____
_____
_____
_____
_____

SPRING

May

Week Three:
Identify Your Purpose as an Educator

Invitation: Building on your reflections from the past two weeks, this week's invitation is to identify your purpose. Why did you choose this profession? What is your deepest why? How would you describe your calling? You can use the "What Is Your Purpose as an Educator?" tool (page 274) if needed.

Monday

Tuesday

Wednesday

The purpose of life is a life of purpose.

—Robert Byrne

Thursday

Friday

Saturday

Sunday

My celebrations:

_____

_____

_____

_____

_____

_____

_____

_____

My challenges:

_____

_____

_____

_____

_____

_____

_____

My considerations
for next week:

_____

_____

_____

_____

_____

_____

_____

SPRING

May

Week Four:
Connect to Your Purpose

Invitation: Reflect on your purpose as an educator (identified in week three) each morning. You might write your purpose on sticky notes or take photos that represent your purpose and post them where you can see them each day. Pay attention to how remembering your purpose each day impacts your overall wellness. You can use the "Connect to Your Purpose as an Educator" tool (page 275) if needed.

Monday

Tuesday

Wednesday

> True happiness . . . is not attained through self-gratification, but through fidelity to a worthy purpose.
>
> —Helen Keller

Thursday

Friday

Saturday

Sunday

End-of-Week Wellness Reflections

My celebrations:

_____

_____

_____

_____

_____

_____

_____

_____

My challenges:

_____

_____

_____

_____

_____

_____

My considerations for next week:

_____

_____

_____

_____

_____

_____

SPRING

May

Week Five:
Share Your Purpose

Invitation: Consider the previous routines around relationships and trust and share your purpose with someone. You might also ask them to share theirs with you. How does it feel to make your purpose public? How does sharing your purpose with others impact your social wellness?

Monday

Tuesday

Wednesday

When you're surrounded by people who share a passionate commitment around a common purpose, anything is possible.

—Howard Schultz

Thursday

Friday

Saturday

Sunday

End-of-Week Wellness Reflections

My celebrations:

_____
_____
_____
_____
_____
_____
_____
_____

My challenges:

_____
_____
_____
_____
_____
_____
_____

My considerations for next week:

_____
_____
_____
_____
_____
_____
_____
_____

SPRING

May

End-of-Month Reflection: Purpose Routines

As May ends, pause for a wellness reflection and respond to the following prompts.

1. Reread the five weekly purpose quotes from this month. Which quote resonated most for you? Why?

_____

_____

_____

_____

2. What did you learn about your purpose this month? What were your celebrations? What were your challenges?

_____

_____

_____

3. Write two *I will* actions regarding your purpose to carry over into summer.

   a. I will:

   _____

   _____

   _____

   _____

   b. I will:

   _____

   _____

   _____

   _____

4. Record any additional thoughts and reflections about your progress this month. How do the routines of relationship, trust, and purpose connect for you? How do you feel when you get off track in one or more of the three social wellness dimensions?

_____

_____

_____

_____

For additional reflection on your purpose routine progress, go to appendix B (page 277) to self-score your current effort and actions.

Notes

_____

_____

_____

_____

_____

_____

_____

_____

_____

_____

_____

_____

_____

_____

_____

_____

_____

_____

_____

_____

_____

_____

_____

_____

_____

_____

_____

_____

SPRING

May

End of Spring: What's Next?

In the words of Booker T. Washington, "I beg of you to remember that wherever our life touches yours, we help or hinder. Wherever your life touches ours, you make us stronger or weaker" (as cited in BlackPast, 2012). There is something spiritual and deep in knowing the power you possess to help, not hinder, others and to make others stronger, more confident, capable, and not weaker.

And, yes, you made it. Another full school year has come and gone. The school year has most likely felt heavy at times and joyful at times. You have a responsibility to be at your best every day. You can simultaneously feel the weight and challenges of your efforts and also the positive impact of your work life on students and colleagues.

You were a steward for the success of every student entrusted to you, and they, in turn, are the beneficiaries of your wellness pursuits. Your weekly wellness efforts this school year have allowed you to move closer to living your best life each day within a profession that serves your greater purpose.

The physical wellness routines of food, movement, and sleep during summer were designed to prepare you for living in a space with relentless energy and enthusiasm. The mental wellness routines during fall were designed for wise and efficient decision making, daily moments of quiet and solitude for internal balance, and the continuous improvement of your self-efficacy to keep you confident, humble, and joyful even on the worst days. The emotional wellness routines in winter were a long journey from awareness to an understanding of mindfulness as a way to sustain your impact on others. And in spring, the social wellness routines of relationship, trust, and purpose were rooted in improving the quality of your connections with others while building high-quality, incredible relationships.

So, now what?

June awaits.

And, once again, your continuous wellness journey begins anew. The next season of your professional life is just ahead. The seasons will repeat as you once again take a trip around the sun.

Notes

_____

_____

SPRING

SPRING

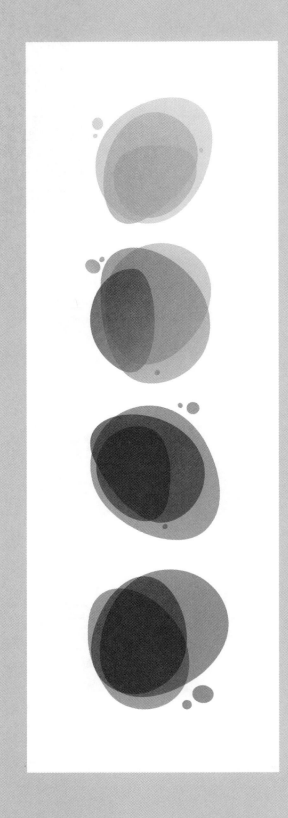

APPENDIX A

JOURNAL TOOLS

There is a difference between interest and commitment. When you're interested in something, you do it only when it's convenient. When you're committed to something you accept no excuses, only results.

—Ken Blanchard

Weekly Tools Index

Note: some weeks don't have tools.

Week	Tool	Invitation	Page
Summer: Physical Wellness Dimension			
June: Food Routines			
One	Healthy Snacks List	Commit to healthier food choices.	230
Two	Water Tracker	Increase your water intake.	231
Three	Healthy Meals Planner	Commit to eating healthy meals.	232
Five	Food Choice and Impact on Mood	Monitor food's effect on mood.	233
July: Movement Routines			
One	Time Spent Sitting and Impact on Mood	Track your sitting time.	234
Two	List of Movement Activities	Find time for your favorite movement activity.	235
Three	Movement Minutes Tracker	Move 150 minutes this week.	236
Four	70,000 Steps Challenge	Find a partner for the 70,000 steps challenge.	237
Five	Movement Activity Tracker	Schedule movement activities.	238
August: Sleep Routines			
One	Sleep Tracker	Track how much you sleep.	239
Two	Wind-Down Routine	Create a wind-down routine.	240
Four	Rest-Time Tracker	Track rest time.	241
Fall: Mental Wellness Dimension			
September: Decision Routines			
One	Decision Tracker	Track decisions.	242
Two	Daily Habit and Routine Commitments	Create daily habits.	243
Four	Brainstorm Activities That Are Just for You	Schedule time for you.	244
Five	Your Daily Affirmations	Develop self-compassion.	245
October: Balance Routines			
One	Busy or Hurried Tracker	Track daily activities.	246
Two	Positive Energy State Tracker	Track your energy.	247
Three	Verbal Communications Tracker	Track verbal communications.	248
Four	Eliminate Inputs and Noise Tracker	Eliminate inputs and noise.	249
Five	Record of Feedback	Ask for feedback.	250
November: Efficacy Routines			
Two	Strengths Challenge	Engage in a strengths challenge.	251
Three	My Vision Board	Create a vision board.	252
Four	Personal TA-DA of Accomplishments	Start a personal résumé.	253

Week	Tool	Invitation	Page
Winter Tools: Emotional Wellness Dimension			
December: Awareness Routines			
One	Emotions Tracker	Track daily emotions.	254
Two	Unpleasant Emotions Response Tracker	Monitor emotional responses.	255
Three	Pleasant Emotions Tracker	Share pleasant emotions.	256
Four	Impact of Your Emotions on Others	Observe emotional impact.	257
Five	Emotional Response Feedback	Get emotional response feedback.	258
January: Understanding Routines			
One	Pleasant Emotion Triggers	Identify pleasant emotion triggers.	259
Two	Unpleasant Emotion Triggers	Identify unpleasant emotion triggers.	260
Four	My Daily Challenge Commitment	Commit to healthy emotional responses.	261
Five	I'm Grateful For	Model healthy emotional responses.	262
February: Mindfulness Routines			
One	React Versus Respond Reflections	Notice react versus respond.	263
Four	Journal Experimenting	Experiment with journaling.	264
Five	Mindful Walking Emotions	Take a mindful walk.	265
Spring Tools: Social Wellness Dimension			
March: Relationship Routines			
One	Thank-You Notes	Write thank-you notes.	266
Three	Gratitude Note	Write a gratitude note.	267
Five	My Inner Circle	Identify inner circle.	268
April: Trust Routines			
Two	Listening Without Interrupting	Listen without interruption.	269
Three	Apology Reflections	Show vulnerability by apologizing.	270
Five	Taking Initiative	Model and build trust.	271
May: Purpose Routines			
One	Who Are You as an Educator?	Discover who you are as an educator.	272
Two	What Are Your Deepest Desires as an Educator?	Consider your desires as an educator.	273
Three	What is Your Purpose as an Educator?	Identify your purpose as an educator.	274
Four	Connect to Your Purpose as an Educator	Connect to your purpose.	275

Healthy Snacks List

Brainstorm healthy snacks you can keep in your pantry and fridge.

Water Tracker

Record how much water you drink each day.

Month: _____

Day 1 ◊◊◊◊◊◊◊◊	Day 16 ◊◊◊◊◊◊◊◊
Day 2 ◊◊◊◊◊◊◊◊	Day 17 ◊◊◊◊◊◊◊◊
Day 3 ◊◊◊◊◊◊◊◊	Day 18 ◊◊◊◊◊◊◊◊
Day 4 ◊◊◊◊◊◊◊◊	Day 19 ◊◊◊◊◊◊◊◊
Day 5 ◊◊◊◊◊◊◊◊	Day 20 ◊◊◊◊◊◊◊◊
Day 6 ◊◊◊◊◊◊◊◊	Day 21 ◊◊◊◊◊◊◊◊
Day 7 ◊◊◊◊◊◊◊◊	Day 22 ◊◊◊◊◊◊◊◊
Day 8 ◊◊◊◊◊◊◊◊	Day 23 ◊◊◊◊◊◊◊◊
Day 9 ◊◊◊◊◊◊◊◊	Day 24 ◊◊◊◊◊◊◊◊
Day 10 ◊◊◊◊◊◊◊◊	Day 25 ◊◊◊◊◊◊◊◊
Day 11 ◊◊◊◊◊◊◊◊	Day 26 ◊◊◊◊◊◊◊◊
Day 12 ◊◊◊◊◊◊◊◊	Day 27 ◊◊◊◊◊◊◊◊
Day 13 ◊◊◊◊◊◊◊◊	Day 28 ◊◊◊◊◊◊◊◊
Day 14 ◊◊◊◊◊◊◊◊	Day 29 ◊◊◊◊◊◊◊◊
Day 15 ◊◊◊◊◊◊◊◊	Day 30 ◊◊◊◊◊◊◊◊

Day 31 ◊◊◊◊◊◊◊◊

Healthy Meals Planner

Brainstorm healthy meals you can have this week.

Sunday	Monday	Tuesday	Shopping List
_____	_____	_____	○ _____
_____	_____	_____	○ _____
_____	_____	_____	○ _____
_____	_____	_____	○ _____
_____	_____	_____	○ _____
_____	_____	_____	○ _____
_____	_____	_____	○ _____
_____	_____	_____	○ _____
_____	_____	_____	○ _____

Wednesday	Thursday	Friday	
_____	_____	_____	○ _____
_____	_____	_____	○ _____
_____	_____	_____	○ _____
_____	_____	_____	○ _____
_____	_____	_____	○ _____
_____	_____	_____	○ _____
_____	_____	_____	○ _____
_____	_____	_____	○ _____
_____	_____	_____	○ _____

Saturday	Notes	
_____		○ _____
_____		○ _____
_____		○ _____
_____		○ _____
_____		○ _____
_____		○ _____
_____		○ _____
_____		○ _____

Food Choice and Impact on Mood

What impact do your food choices have on your mood? Track the food you eat, circle how it makes you feel, and record any notes about its impact on your mood.

Day	Food	Mood Tracker	Notes on Impact on Mood
		☺ ☺ 😐 🙁 ☹	
		☺ ☺ 😐 🙁 ☹	
		☺ ☺ 😐 🙁 ☹	
		☺ ☺ 😐 🙁 ☹	
		☺ ☺ 😐 🙁 ☹	
		☺ ☺ 😐 🙁 ☹	
		☺ ☺ 😐 🙁 ☹	
		☺ ☺ 😐 🙁 ☹	
		☺ ☺ 😐 🙁 ☹	
		☺ ☺ 😐 🙁 ☹	
		☺ ☺ 😐 🙁 ☹	
		☺ ☺ 😐 🙁 ☹	
		☺ ☺ 😐 🙁 ☹	
		☺ ☺ 😐 🙁 ☹	
		☺ ☺ 😐 🙁 ☹	
		☺ ☺ 😐 🙁 ☹	
		☺ ☺ 😐 🙁 ☹	
		☺ ☺ 😐 🙁 ☹	
		☺ ☺ 😐 🙁 ☹	
		☺ ☺ 😐 🙁 ☹	

Time Spent Sitting and Impact on Mood

Track how much time you spend sitting during the day and circle how it impacts your mood

SUMMER

July

	Time Spent Sitting	Impact on Mood
Sunday	Morning: _____ Afternoon: _____ Evening: _____	☺ ☺ 😐 ☹ ☹ ☺ ☺ 😐 ☹ ☹ ☺ ☺ 😐 ☹ ☹
Monday	Morning: _____ Afternoon: _____ Evening: _____	☺ ☺ 😐 ☹ ☹ ☺ ☺ 😐 ☹ ☹ ☺ ☺ 😐 ☹ ☹
Tuesday	Morning: _____ Afternoon: _____ Evening: _____	☺ ☺ 😐 ☹ ☹ ☺ ☺ 😐 ☹ ☹ ☺ ☺ 😐 ☹ ☹
Wednesday	Morning: _____ Afternoon: _____ Evening: _____	☺ ☺ 😐 ☹ ☹ ☺ ☺ 😐 ☹ ☹ ☺ ☺ 😐 ☹ ☹
Thursday	Morning: _____ Afternoon: _____ Evening: _____	☺ ☺ 😐 ☹ ☹ ☺ ☺ 😐 ☹ ☹ ☺ ☺ 😐 ☹ ☹
Friday	Morning: _____ Afternoon: _____ Evening: _____	☺ ☺ 😐 ☹ ☹ ☺ ☺ 😐 ☹ ☹ ☺ ☺ 😐 ☹ ☹
Saturday	Morning: _____ Afternoon: _____ Evening: _____	☺ ☺ 😐 ☹ ☹ ☺ ☺ 😐 ☹ ☹ ☺ ☺ 😐 ☹ ☹

List of Movement Activities

Brainstorm movement activities you enjoy.

_____   _____
_____   _____
_____   _____
_____   _____
_____   _____
_____   _____
_____   _____
_____   _____
_____   _____
_____   _____
_____   _____
_____   _____
_____   _____
_____   _____
_____   _____
_____   _____
_____   _____
_____   _____
_____   _____
_____   _____
_____   _____
_____   _____
_____   _____

Movement Minutes Tracker

Record how many minutes of movement activity you engage in
every day this month (goal is 150 minutes for the week).

Month: _____   Goal: _____

Day 1	Day 16
Day 2	Day 17
Day 3	Day 18
Day 4	Day 19
Day 5	Day 20
Day 6	Day 21
Day 7	Day 22
Day 8	Day 23
Day 9	Day 24
Day 10	Day 25
Day 11	Day 26
Day 12	Day 27
Day 13	Day 28
Day 14	Day 29
Day 15	Day 30/31

70,000 Steps Challenge

Record your number of steps each day this week (goal is 70,000 steps for the week). If walking is not possible, consider other forms of movement such as hand cycling, water aerobics, swimming, yoga, or stretching and record your progress each day.

Month: _____   Goal for Four Weeks: _____

Day 1	
Day 2	
Day 3	
Day 4	
Day 5	
Day 6	
Day 7	
Total steps	

Day 15	
Day 16	
Day 17	
Day 18	
Day 19	
Day 20	
Day 21	
Total steps	

Day 8	
Day 9	
Day 10	
Day 11	
Day 12	
Day 13	
Day 14	
Total steps	

Day 22	
Day 23	
Day 24	
Day 25	
Day 26	
Day 27	
Day 28	
Total steps	

Movement Activity Tracker

Be intentional about scheduling movement activities each day. Use this tracker to indicate your activity, time spent on the activity, and your level of intensity (high, medium, or low).

	Activity	Time Spent on Activity	Level of Intensity
Sunday			
Monday			
Tuesday			
Wednesday			
Thursday			
Friday			
Saturday			

Sleep Tracker

Record the number of hours you sleep each night.

	Sunday	Monday	Tuesday	Wednesday	Thursday	Friday	Saturday
Week One							
Week Two							
Week Three							
Week Four							
Week Five							

	Sunday	Monday	Tuesday	Wednesday	Thursday	Friday	Saturday
Week One							
Week Two							
Week Three							
Week Four							
Week Five							

	Sunday	Monday	Tuesday	Wednesday	Thursday	Friday	Saturday
Week One							
Week Two							
Week Three							
Week Four							
Week Five							

Wind-Down Routine

Create your wind-down routine (for example, turning off all electronics at a certain time, taking a bath, journaling, reading, or drinking a cup of decaffeinated tea).

7 p.m. to 8 p.m.

8 p.m. to 9 p.m.

9 p.m. to 10 p.m.

10 p.m. to 11 p.m.

The Educator Wellness Plan Book and Journal © 2023 Solution Tree Press

SolutionTree.com • Visit **go.SolutionTree.com/educatorwellness** to download this free reproducible.

240 — THE EDUCATOR WELLNESS PLAN BOOK & JOURNAL

Rest-Time Tracker

Record how much rest time you get each day.

	Sunday	Monday	Tuesday	Wednesday	Thursday	Friday	Saturday
Week One							
Week Two							
Week Three							
Week Four							
Week Five							

	Sunday	Monday	Tuesday	Wednesday	Thursday	Friday	Saturday
Week One							
Week Two							
Week Three							
Week Four							
Week Five							

	Sunday	Monday	Tuesday	Wednesday	Thursday	Friday	Saturday
Week One							
Week Two							
Week Three							
Week Four							
Week Five							

Decision Tracker

Track the number of decisions you made during the school day
by crossing out one box for each decision.

Sept.

F A L L

Monday

Tuesday

Wednesday

Thursday

Friday

Monday

Tuesday

Wednesday

Thursday

Friday

Daily Habit and Routine Commitments

Use the following lines to brainstorm a list of daily habits and routines.

_____

_____

_____

_____

_____

_____

_____

_____

_____

_____

_____

_____

_____

_____

_____

_____

_____

_____

_____

_____

_____

_____

_____

_____

_____

_____

_____

_____

_____

_____

_____

FALL Sept.

Brainstorm Activities That Are Just for You

Use the following lines to brainstorm some activities that are just for you.
Then schedule them in your calendar.

Your Daily Affirmations

Use the following lines to brainstorm some affirmation
statements to help develop your self-compassion.

Busy or Hurried Tracker

Track how your daily activities make you feel either *busy* (thriving, fully present, in-demand, satisfied, and loving the action) or *hurried* (anxious, unable to be fully present with others, not enough time, physically and emotionally exhausted).

Activity	
	☐ Busy ☐ Hurried
	☐ Busy ☐ Hurried
	☐ Busy ☐ Hurried
	☐ Busy ☐ Hurried
	☐ Busy ☐ Hurried
	☐ Busy ☐ Hurried
	☐ Busy ☐ Hurried
	☐ Busy ☐ Hurried
	☐ Busy ☐ Hurried
	☐ Busy ☐ Hurried
	☐ Busy ☐ Hurried
	☐ Busy ☐ Hurried
	☐ Busy ☐ Hurried
	☐ Busy ☐ Hurried

FALL

Oct.

Positive Energy State Tracker

Mark an X on the line to indicate your current energy level. Is it high-positive or low-positive?

	Morning	Afternoon	Evening
Day 1	low high positive	low high positive	low high positive
Day 2	low high positive	low high positive	low high positive
Day 3	low high positive	low high positive	low high positive
Day 4	low high positive	low high positive	low high positive
Day 5	low high positive	low high positive	low high positive
Day 6	low high positive	low high positive	low high positive
Day 7	low high positive	low high positive	low high positive

FALL   Oct.

Verbal Communications Tracker

Track your verbal communications. How often do your words reflect positivity or negativity?

Date	Words or Phrase	Positive	Negative

FALL
Oct.

Eliminate Inputs and Noise Tracker

Make time for eliminating inputs and noise by marking it on your calendar.
Reflect on how you feel during this time.

Time of Day	Location	Noise or Input Eliminated	Duration	How Do I Feel?

F A L L · Oct.

Record of Feedback

What do your colleagues and family members say about you on most days? Ask for feedback.

Name of person giving feedback: _____

Do I demonstrate high energy?	
Do I demonstrate a well-balanced, professional, and joyful self?	
Do I demonstrate confidence?	
Do I demonstrate hopefulness?	
Do I demonstrate happiness?	

Strengths Challenge

List ten strengths that you are proud to have.

1. _____   6. _____

2. _____   7. _____

3. _____   8. _____

4. _____   9. _____

5. _____   10. _____

As the week goes on, and throughout the school year, list more strengths as you think of them.

_____   _____

_____   _____

_____   _____

_____   _____

_____   _____

_____   _____

_____   _____

FALL

Nov.

My Vision Board

Set specific goals to help you work toward achieving them.

Health goals	• • • •
Financial goals	• • • •
Relationship goals	• • • •
Career goals	• • • •
Education goals	• • • •
Travel goals	• • • •

Personal TA-DA of Accomplishments

Write down the accomplishments you have had over the course of your life.
Add to the list every time you achieve another accomplishment.

Accomplishment	Date Accomplished

FALL

Nov.

Emotions Tracker

Track your daily emotions.

Day of the Week	Emotion Experienced

Dec.

WINTER

Unpleasant Emotions Response Tracker

Record your responses to unpleasant emotions you experience
or that others express toward you this week.

Unpleasant Emotion	Emotional Response

WINTER Dec.

Pleasant Emotions Tracker

Record the pleasant emotions you experienced this week,
and how you shared them with others.

Pleasant Emotion	How I Shared With Others

Dec.

WINTER

Impact of Your Emotions on Others

Describe a moment from each day when you noticed the impact of your positive emotions on the learning, perseverance, or effort of others.

Emotion Experienced	Time	Location	Who Did It Impact?

WINTER Dec.

Emotional Response Feedback

How do your daily emotional responses impact others? Ask one student, colleague, friend, or family member: "Are my daily emotional responses generally positive toward others? Why or why not?" Record their answer and then reflect on it.

Reflection

Pleasant Emotion Triggers

Identify events that trigger your happier and more excited emotions.

Pleasant Emotion	Event or Situation That Triggered It

WINTER
Jan.

Unpleasant Emotion Triggers

Identify events that trigger unpleasant emotions.

Unpleasant Emotion	Event or Situation That Triggered It

WINTER

Jan.

My Daily Challenge Commitment

Identify situations that cause you to experience unpleasant emotions
(for example, driving during rush hour, reading a social media post, and so on)
and make it a challenge to not react negatively.

WINTER

Jan.

I'm Grateful For

Write about people, places, moments, or activities in your daily life
that make you happy and make you smile. Reflect each day on how you can
model more healthy emotional responses toward others.

WINTER

Jan.

React Versus Respond Reflections

Notice when you react versus when you respond to your emotions
and the emotions of others this week.

Date	Situation	I Responded	I Reacted

WINTER

Feb.

The Educator Wellness Plan Book and Journal © 2023 Solution Tree Press
SolutionTree.com • Visit **go.SolutionTree.com/educatorwellness** to download this free reproducible.

Journal Experimenting

Experiment with journaling. Try a brain dump, where you write whatever you're thinking without worrying about editing yourself or your writing. You can also doodle or color.

Mindful Walking Emotions

Take a mindful walk and record emotions before and after the walk.

Date	Before-Walk Emotions	After-Walk Emotions

WINTER

Feb.

Thank-You Notes

Decide who you can write thank-you notes to this week.

Gratitude Note

Brainstorm some ideas for a gratitude note. What are some key points you'd like to put in the letter to show your gratitude?

_____
_____
_____
_____
_____
_____
_____
_____
_____
_____
_____
_____
_____
_____
_____
_____
_____
_____
_____
_____
_____
_____
_____
_____
_____
_____

SPRING · March

My Inner Circle

Make a list of all colleagues, friends, and family members in your closest inner circle who challenge and inspire you.
Then, list three intentional actions you can take to spend more time with them.

Who Challenges and Inspires You?	Intentional Actions to Spend More Time With Them

March

SPRING

Listening Without Interrupting

How can I show that I am listening? This week, listen to others without interrupting and commit to talking less. Reflect on your experiences with listening here.

_____

_____

_____

_____

_____

_____

_____

_____

_____

_____

_____

_____

_____

_____

_____

_____

_____

_____

_____

_____

_____

_____

_____

_____

_____

_____

_____

_____

_____

SPRING

April

Apology Reflections

Practice apologizing to a student, colleague, friend, or family member.

Who I Apologized To	How It Made Me Feel

Taking Initiative

Record any current issue or challenging situation, and then how you can take action to help students or colleagues solve the problem.

_____
_____
_____
_____
_____
_____
_____
_____
_____
_____
_____
_____
_____
_____
_____
_____
_____
_____
_____
_____
_____
_____
_____
_____
_____
_____
_____
_____
_____
_____
_____
_____
_____
_____
_____

SPRING

April

Who Are You as An Educator?

Consider who you are as an educator. Use your mindfulness routines to pause and reflect. Record any sensations, images, feelings, or thoughts that come to you.

_____

_____

_____

_____

_____

_____

_____

_____

_____

_____

_____

_____

_____

_____

_____

_____

_____

_____

_____

_____

_____

Write who you are as an educator in ten words or fewer.

_____

_____

_____

SPRING

May

What Are Your Deepest Desires as an Educator?

Consider your desires as an educator. Again, using your mindfulness routines,
pause and reflect. What is it that you want as an educator?
Record any sensations, images, feelings, or thoughts to come to you.

_____

_____

_____

_____

_____

_____

_____

_____

_____

_____

_____

_____

_____

_____

_____

_____

_____

_____

_____

_____

_____

_____

_____

_____

_____

_____

_____

_____

SPRING

May

What Is Your Purpose as an Educator?

Why did you choose this profession? What is your deepest why?
How would you describe your calling?

_____

_____

_____

_____

_____

_____

_____

_____

_____

_____

_____

_____

_____

_____

_____

_____

_____

_____

_____

_____

_____

_____

_____

_____

_____

_____

_____

_____

_____

_____

_____

_____

SPRING

May

Connect to Your Purpose as an Educator

Reflect on your purpose as an educator each morning this week.

Monday

_____
_____
_____

Tuesday

_____
_____
_____

Wednesday

_____
_____
_____

Thursday

_____
_____
_____

Friday

_____
_____
_____

Saturday

_____
_____
_____

Sunday

_____
_____
_____

SPRING

May

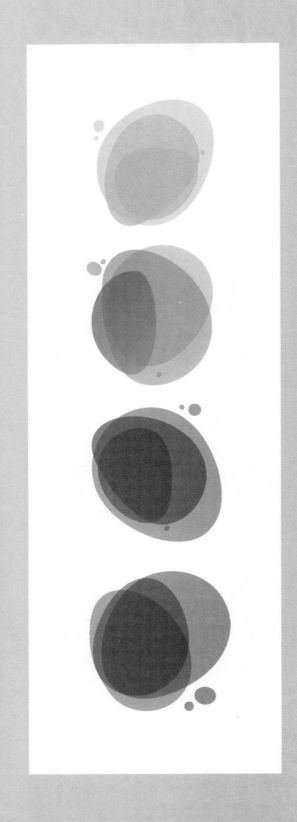

APPENDIX B

WELLNESS SOLUTIONS FOR EDUCATORS

RATING, REFLECTING, GOAL SETTING, PLANNING,
AND PROGRESS MONITORING PROTOCOL

Wellness Solutions for Educators *Rating, Reflecting, Goal Setting, Planning, and Progress Monitoring* Protocol

Here is a guide for how to use the eight figures and two parts of appendix B: *Rating, Reflecting, Goal Setting, Planning, and Progress Monitoring* protocol.

Part I: Rating and Reflecting—Figures B.1–B.4

This section of the protocol asks you to rate and reflect on your current state of well-being and wellness for each of the four dimensions and three corresponding routines discussed in the book and listed as part of the Wellness Solutions for Educators framework. This appendix originally appeared in *Educator Wellness: A Guide for Sustaining Physical, Mental, Emotional, and Social Well-Being* (Kanold & Boogren, 2022).

Figure B.1: Educator wellness self-rating and reflection—*Physical wellness routines.*

Figure B.2: Educator wellness self-rating and reflection—*Mental wellness routines.*

Figure B.3: Educator wellness self-rating and reflection—*Emotional wellness routines.*

Figure B.4: Educator wellness self-rating and reflection—*Social wellness routines.*

You will notice each figure represents one wellness dimension and its three corresponding routines, followed by six yes or no action statements for each routine.

Use the following process to complete each rating and reflecting protocol provided in figures B.1–B.4.

1. Read the six yes or no action statements for each routine. Check the box if your response is yes; leave the box blank if your response is no.

2. For each routine, give yourself a rating score between 1–4 in the space provided. You can use a marker or a pen to highlight your score.

3. Use the bottom space of figures B.1–B.4 to identify your strongest routine for that corresponding dimension and to identify your wellness routine most in need of improvement. Use the space to briefly comment your reflection.

Part II: Planning, Goal Setting, and Progress Monitoring—Figures B.5–B.8

This section of appendix B asks you to plan for strategies and actions using figures B.5 and B.6 and then use the progress monitoring tools provided in figures B.7 and B.8 to measure your ongoing wellness improvement. You can use figures B.5–B.8 to help you meet goals for wellness proficiency (ratings of 3.5 or higher) with each routine you identified for improvement.

Figure B.5: Educator wellness planning tool—Routines that are strengths.

Figure B.6: Educator wellness planning tool—Routines for improvement.

Figures B.5 and B.6 are planning tools with which you identify specific strategies and actions. In figure B.5, you write about strategies you use for the routines that represent areas of strength for you. Write *I do . . .* statements as you consider why you are successful for the identified routine. In figure B.6, you write about strategies and actions you need to take to become more proficient in each identified routine. You write these statements as actions, starting with *I will . . . .*

Figure B.7: Educator wellness goal setting and progress monitoring tool—*Physical and mental wellness progress monitoring.*

Figure B.8: Educator wellness goal setting and progress monitoring tool—*Emotional and social wellness progress monitoring.*

Use figures B.7 and B.8 as progress monitoring tools for each dimension of educator wellness. Notice you can self-rate from 1.0–4.0 in increments of 0.5. As you check in on your weekly progress, be sure to indicate the date of your progress check-in so you can observe your progress over time.

Consider sharing your results in figures B.7 and B.8 with a trusted colleague or team. Perhaps establish a team wellness goal in addition to your own wellness goals.

Physical Wellness Dimension

Directions: Complete your *physical wellness* dimension self-rating. If your response to the prompt is yes, check the box. Then rank yourself 1–4 for each routine (consider your number of yes responses), followed by identifying your strengths and routines for possible improvement.

Food routines: Consider what and when you eat and drink, and how well you hydrate during the day.			
☐ I monitor my food choices most days.			
☐ My food choices energize me.			
☐ I stay hydrated throughout the day.			
☐ I take time to eat breakfast and lunch during my workday.			
☐ I am able to eat without distractions.			
☐ I monitor how my food choices impact my mood.			
1	**2**	**3**	**4**

Movement routines: Consider what, when, and how well you move during the day.			
☐ I monitor how much I sit or stand each day.			
☐ I monitor my number of steps during the day.			
☐ I monitor how my movement impacts my mood.			
☐ I feel energized most days.			
☐ I take brain breaks during my day (perhaps with students).			
☐ I practice movement routines with my colleagues or students.			
1	**2**	**3**	**4**

Sleep routines: Consider how much sleep and rest you get during each twenty-four-hour cycle.			
☐ I monitor the hourly amount of my daily sleep.			
☐ I feel rested most days when at work.			
☐ My sleep positively impacts my mood and behavior.			
☐ I use a common daily sleep routine.			
☐ I take time to rest during the day without guilt.			
☐ I support students or colleagues who may not be getting enough sleep.			
1	**2**	**3**	**4**

Self-Rating: 1 = Beginning; 2 = Implementing; 3 = Embracing; 4 = Modeling

Self-Reflection Plan Of these three physical wellness routines:

Which routine is your greatest strength, and why?	Which routine most needs your attention, and why?

Figure B.1: Educator wellness self-rating and reflection—Physical wellness routines.

Visit **go.SolutionTree.com/educatorwellness** for a free reproducible version of this figure.

Mental Wellness Dimension

Directions: Complete your *mental wellness* dimension self-rating. If your response to the prompt is yes, check the box. Then rank yourself 1–4 for each routine (consider your number of yes responses), followed by identifying your strengths and routines for possible improvement.

Decision routines: Consider how well you reduce, automate, and regulate the decisions you make each day to avoid decision fatigue.				**Balance routines:** Consider how well you live a busy, high-energy, well-balanced day-to-day work life and avoid prolonged stress.				**Efficacy routines:** Consider how well you build your confidence and competence and improve your work-life capabilities each day.			
☐ I know the number of educational decisions I make each day. ☐ I automate when and how I do certain work-related tasks. ☐ I avoid being exhausted from the volume of my daily decisions. ☐ I excel at time management. ☐ I know what self-compassion is and practice it. ☐ I self-regulate the positive or negative impact of my decisions on others.				☐ I stay busy without becoming hurried or exhausted. ☐ I fully engage in a high-positive-energy work life each day. ☐ I avoid cynical or negative behaviors. ☐ I commit time for silence and quiet from the daily noise of life. ☐ I maintain positive low-energy time for self-reflection and improvement. ☐ I demonstrate a high-energy, well-balanced professional and joyful life for others to observe.				☐ I know how to improve my self-efficacy. ☐ I practice specific routines to overcome the adversity I encounter each week. ☐ I reframe my doubts into challenges and as opportunities for my growth. ☐ I am confident in my ability to help every child learn. ☐ I continuously seek to improve my competency and knowledge. ☐ I seek evidence of student success as one measure toward my self-efficacy.			
1	2	3	4	1	2	3	4	1	2	3	4

Self-Rating: 1 = Beginning; 2 = Implementing; 3 = Embracing; 4 = Modeling

Self-Reflection Plan Of these three mental wellness routines:

Which routine is your greatest strength, and why?	Which routine most needs your attention, and why?

Figure B.2: Educator wellness self-rating and reflection—Mental wellness routines.

Visit **go.SolutionTree.com/educatorwellness** for a free reproducible version of this figure.

Emotional Wellness Dimension

Directions: Complete your ***emotional wellness*** dimension self-rating. If your response to the prompt is yes, check the box. Then rank yourself 1–4 for each routine (consider your number of yes responses), followed by identifying your strengths and routines for possible improvement.

Awareness routines: Consider how well you identify, keep track of, and respond to your daily emotions.

- ☐ I pay attention to my emotions each day.
- ☐ I respond positively to my strong, unpleasant emotions like sadness or anger.
- ☐ I share my strong, pleasant emotions like happiness and tenderness with others.
- ☐ I know how my negative emotional reactions impact student cognition.
- ☐ I am aware of how my emotional responses impact my colleagues.
- ☐ I collect data on my emotional responses to events and to other people.

1	2	3	4

Understanding routines: Consider the why behind your emotions and how well you reflect on your responses to different emotions.

- ☐ I connect my emotional state to my work-life events and experiences.
- ☐ I know the emotional triggers for my more unpleasant emotions.
- ☐ I take the time to identify patterns related to my daily emotions.
- ☐ I recognize how different emotions can show up in my body.
- ☐ I generally respond positively to others when unpleasant emotions surface.
- ☐ I model healthy emotional responses for students and colleagues.

1	2	3	4

Mindfulness routines: Consider how well you use mindfulness practices to respond rather than react to your strong and more unpleasant emotions.

- ☐ I use available strategies to effectively respond to my strong emotions.
- ☐ I thoughtfully respond more than I negatively react to my daily emotions.
- ☐ I thoughtfully respond more than I negatively react to others' emotions.
- ☐ I engage in daily mindful breathing, meditation, or journaling practices.
- ☐ I model a daily positive emotional response toward students and colleagues.
- ☐ I take time to reflect daily on my emotional impact on others.

1	2	3	4

Self-Rating: 1 = Beginning; 2 = Implementing; 3 = Embracing; 4 = Modeling

Self-Reflection Plan Of these three emotional wellness routines:

Which routine is your greatest strength, and why?

Which routine most needs your attention, and why?

Figure B.3: Educator wellness self-rating and reflection—Emotional wellness routines.

Visit **go.SolutionTree.com/educatorwellness** for a free reproducible version of this figure.

Social Wellness Dimension

Directions: Complete your *social wellness* dimension self-rating. If your response to the prompt is yes, check the box. Then rank yourself 1–4 for each routine (consider your number of yes responses), followed by identifying your strengths and routines for possible improvement.

Relationship routines: Consider how well you and your colleagues build strong relationships and social connections together.				**Trust routines:** Consider how well you build daily work-life routines of vulnerability and deep listening without judgment of others.				**Purpose routines:** Consider how your daily work life feeds into your greater purpose and helps you find meaning and joy in your work life.			

Relationship routines:
- ☐ I know my well-being is connected to my daily effort to enhance the lives of others.
- ☐ I know close positive relationships are a predictor of success in life.
- ☐ I initiate strong, positive relationships with colleagues.
- ☐ I work with colleagues and students to create cultural norms of belonging and inclusion.
- ☐ I work with my colleagues to improve my communication skills.
- ☐ I seek to build a social support network of colleagues and friends.

Trust routines:
- ☐ I have colleagues I trust.
- ☐ I practice deep listening without judgment of others.
- ☐ I am able to be vulnerable with colleagues by asking for help.
- ☐ I practice vulnerability with my colleagues in order to build trust.
- ☐ I have colleagues and friends I often seek for help, wisdom, or advice.
- ☐ I actively seek to model and build trust with students and colleagues.

Purpose routines:
- ☐ My career is my vocation—part of something bigger than myself.
- ☐ My role as an educator is something I feel compelled to do with my life, no matter the challenges.
- ☐ My role as an educator connects me to my greater purpose.
- ☐ I know and understand the contributions I am making toward the growth of others.
- ☐ I know my improvement in physical, mental, and emotional routines impacts my overall social wellness and purpose.

Relationship				Trust				Purpose			
1	2	3	4	1	2	3	4	1	2	3	4

Self-Rating: 1 = Beginning; 2 = Implementing; 3 = Embracing; 4 = Modeling

Self-Reflection Plan Of these three social wellness routines:

Which routine is your greatest strength, and why?	Which routine most needs your attention, and why?

Figure B.4: Educator wellness self-rating and reflection—Social wellness routines.

Visit **go.SolutionTree.com/educatorwellness** for a free reproducible version of this figure.

Educator Wellness Planning Tool — Strengths

Directions: Based on your self-rating responses from figures B.1–B.4 (pages 279–282), identify the routines that are currently strengths for you here, in figure B.5. In the space provided, write one strategy that works for you. Start it with the phrase *I do* . . . . .

Physical Wellness	Food Routine Strategies	Movement Routine Strategies	Sleep Routine Strategies
Mental Wellness	Decision Routine Strategies	Balance Routine Strategies	Efficacy Routine Strategies
Emotional Wellness	Awareness Routine Strategies	Understanding Routine Strategies	Mindfulness Routine Strategies
Social Wellness	Relationship Routine Strategies	Trust Routine Strategies	Purpose Routine Strategies

Figure B.5: Educator wellness planning tool—*Routines that are strengths.*

Visit **go.SolutionTree.com/educatorwellness** for a free reproducible version of this figure.

Educator Wellness Planning Tool – Routines for Improvement

Directions: Based on your self-rating responses from figures B.1–B.4 (pages 279–282), identify the routines that are currently in need of improvement for you here, in figure B.6. In the space provided, write one action to get started. Lead with the phrase *I will* . . . .

Physical **Wellness**	Food Routine Strategies	Movement Routine Strategies	Sleep Routine Strategies
Mental **Wellness**	Decision Routine Strategies	Balance Routine Strategies	Efficacy Routine Strategies
Emotional **Wellness**	Awareness Routine Strategies	Understanding Routine Strategies	Mindfulness Routine Strategies
Social **Wellness**	Relationship Routine Strategies	Trust Routine Strategies	Purpose Routine Strategies

Figure B.6: Educator wellness planning tool—*Routines for improvement.*

Visit **go.SolutionTree.com/educatorwellness** for a free reproducible version of this figure.

Educator Wellness Goal Setting, Planning, and Progress Monitoring

Directions: Based on your self-rating and planning responses from figures B.1–B.6 (pages 279–284), identify *physical and mental* wellness routines to measure your progress and proficiency. Be sure to indicate the date for each progress check. Fill in or X the boxes.

Physical Wellness

Food Routine Progress

Date	1.0	1.5	2.0	2.5	3.0	3.5	4.0

Movement Routine Progress

Date	1.0	1.5	2.0	2.5	3.0	3.5	4.0

Sleep Routine Progress

Date	1.0	1.5	2.0	2.5	3.0	3.5	4.0

Mental Wellness

Decision Routine Progress

Date	1.0	1.5	2.0	2.5	3.0	3.5	4.0

Balance Routine Progress

Date	1.0	1.5	2.0	2.5	3.0	3.5	4.0

Efficacy Routine Progress

Date	1.0	1.5	2.0	2.5	3.0	3.5	4.0

Figure B.7: Educator wellness goal setting and planning tool—*Physical and mental wellness progress monitoring.*

Visit **go.SolutionTree.com/educatorwellness** for a free reproducible version of this figure.

Educator Wellness Goal Setting, Planning, and Progress Monitoring

Directions: Based on your self-rating and planning responses from figures B.1–B.6 (pages 279–284), identify *emotional and social* wellness routines to measure your progress and proficiency. Be sure to indicate the date for each progress check. Fill in or X the boxes.

Emotional Wellness

Awareness Routine Progress

Date	1.0	1.5	2.0	2.5	3.0	3.5	4.0

Understanding Routine Progress

Date	1.0	1.5	2.0	2.5	3.0	3.5	4.0

Mindfulness Routine Progress

Date	1.0	1.5	2.0	2.5	3.0	3.5	4.0

Social Wellness

Relationship Routine Progress

Date	1.0	1.5	2.0	2.5	3.0	3.5	4.0

Trust Routine Progress

Date	1.0	1.5	2.0	2.5	3.0	3.5	4.0

Purpose Routine Progress

Date	1.0	1.5	2.0	2.5	3.0	3.5	4.0

Figure B.8: Educator wellness goal setting and planning tool—*Emotional and social wellness progress monitoring.*

Visit **go.SolutionTree.com/educatorwellness** for a free reproducible version of this figure.

References and
Resources

Bandura, A. (2012). On the functional properties of perceived self-efficacy revisited. *Journal of Management, 38*(1), 9–44. https://journals.sagepub.com/doi/full/10.1177/0149206311410606

BlackPast. (2012, March 15). *(1896) Booker T. Washington, "Address to the Harvard alumni dinner"*. Accessed at www.blackpast.org/african-american-history/1896-booker-t-washington-address-harvard-alumni-dinner on April 19, 2021.

Brackett, M. A., & Simmons, D. (2015). Emotions matter. *Educational Leadership, 73*(2), 22–27.

Goldberg, G., & Houser, R. (2017, July 19). *Battling decision fatigue* [Blog post]. Accessed at www.edutopia.org/blog/battling-decision-fatigue-gravity-goldberg-renee-houser on February 7, 2023.

Goleman, D. (2006). *Social intelligence: The new science of human relationships*. New York: Bantam Books.

Harvard Health Publishing. (2022, May 15). *How much water should you drink?* Accessed at www.health.harvard.edu/staying-healthy/how-much-water-should-you-drink on March 14, 2023.

Institute for Health and Human Potential. (n.d.). *The meaning of emotional intelligence*. Accessed at www.ihhp.com/meaning-of-emotional-intelligence on December 1st, 2022.

Kanold, T. D., & Boogren, T. H. (2021). *Educator wellness: A guide for sustaining physical, mental, emotional, and social well-being*. Bloomington, IN: Solution Tree Press.

Langshur, E., & Klemp, N. (2016). *Start here: Master the lifelong habit of wellbeing*. New York: Gallery Books.

Mlodinow, L. (2022). *Emotional: How feelings shape our thinking*. New York: Pantheon Books.

Newsom, R. (2023, March 3). *Diet, exercise, and sleep*. Accessed at www.sleepfoundation.org/physical-health/diet-exercise-sleep on March 16, 2023.

Rath, T. (2013). *Eat move sleep: How small choices lead to big changes.* Arlington, VA: Missionday.

Seppälä, E., & King, M. (2017, June 29). *Burnout at work isn't just about exhaustion. It's also about loneliness.* Accessed at https://hbr.org/2017/06/burnout-at-work-isnt -just-about-exhaustion-its-also-about-loneliness on February 7, 2023.

Tomlinson, C. A., & Sousa, D. A. (2020, May 1). *The sciences of teaching.* Accessed at www.ascd.org/el/articles/the-sciences-of-teaching on March 14, 2023.

Turkle, S. (2012). *Connected, but alone?* [Video file]. TED Conferences. Accessed at www.ted.com/talks/sherry_turkle_connected_but_alone/transcript on December 1, 2022.

Yale School of Medicine. (n.d.). *Yale Center for Emotional Intelligence (YCEI).* Accessed at https://medicine.yale.edu/childstudy/services/community-and-schools -programs/center-for-emotional-intelligence on February 9, 2023.

Zak, P. J. (2017). The neuroscience of trust. *Harvard Business Review.* Accessed at https://hbr.org/2017/01/the-neuroscience-of-trust on December 1, 2022.